AMMO

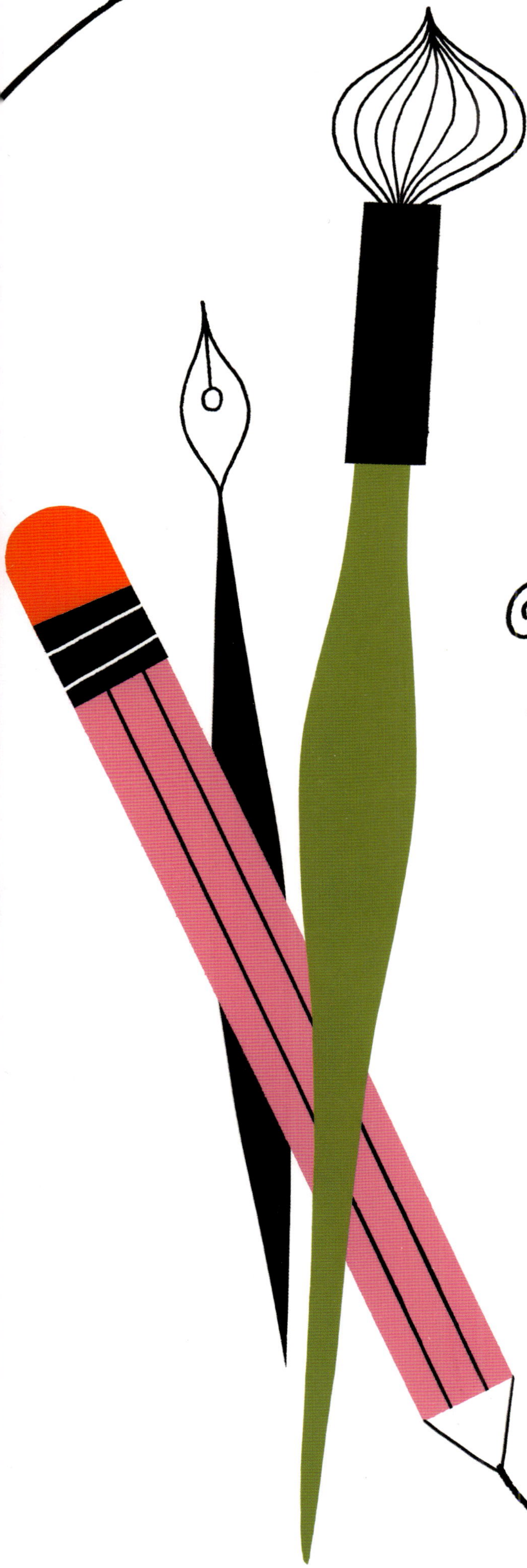

Mid-Century Modern Women

In the Visual Arts

Illustrated by Ellen Surrey

Edited by Gloria Fowler

Introduction

When I first came across Ellen Surrey's delightful illustration of Peggy Moffitt, it was love at first sight. The connection was twofold. First, Ellen Surrey is an incredibly talented, young illustrator who is a recent graduate of the renowned Art Center College of Design, which coincidentally is also my alma mater and a place I called home in the twenty years I taught there. Secondly, Peggy Moffitt is not only one of the most iconic fashion models of the mid-twentieth century but also a dear family friend. Her late husband, the celebrated photographer William Claxton, was my husband Steve Crist's close friend and mentor. In fact, one of our favorite vintage photographs of Peggy by Bill hangs in our home.

During the 1960s, Peggy Moffitt caused a sensation as the model and muse for Rudi Gernreich's bold and graphic clothing designs, perhaps none more so than the monokini, the topless swimsuit she so elegantly modeled. Peggy's background in dance gave a fluidity to her movements that was captured on film by William Claxton. Together they created what is considered the first fashion video: *Basic Black*, which is now in the permanent collection at MoMA in New York. Coupled with her Kabuki-style makeup she created herself and her geometric Vidal Sassoon haircut, Peggy invented a look all her own. Indeed, Peggy was more than just a model; she was an aesthetic collaborator and communicator.

This made me think about all the other amazing, creative women from this era that I adored—women like Ray Eames, who I came to admire even more so after designing and editing the monograph *Eames: Beautiful Details*. I realized there were so many more remarkable women from this era who were sometimes overlooked, and I knew right away that Ellen and I should create a book together that celebrated women in the visual arts from the mid-twentieth century. It felt like serendipity, and the result of our collaboration is this exhibit-in-a-book: an eclectic list of twenty-five real-life heroines across multiple disciplines whose work and whose lives continue to inspire today. From Edith Head to Edith Heath, from Eva Hesse to Eva Zeisel, the twenty-five talented women featured here are influential for both their artistry and determination. Ellen Surrey's exquisite portraits of these women are accompanied by quotes from each of them, imparting both wit and wisdom from their own life experiences.

Mid-twentieth-century modernism, long celebrated for its much-lauded designs by mostly male designers, architects, and artists, was also a time of groundbreaking work in the visual arts by extraordinarily talented women. Predominantly focused on the 1940s to the 1960s, with the influence of the Bauhaus beforehand and foreshadowing the emergence of the feminist movement afterwards, this book celebrates an era that saw unprecedented accomplishments in the arts by women. In architecture, illustration, animation, textile design, graphic design, industrial design, furniture design, painting, sculpture, ceramics, costume design, and fashion, every one of these unique women pursued her own distinct vision in fields that were largely underrepresented by and inaccessible to women. This book shines the spotlight on a diverse sampling of talented women across all of these disciplines, who created wonderful works with wit and willfulness. Amongst the women featured here are some of the most recognizable names in the arts from this time period, such as fashion maven Coco Chanel, and painters Frida Kahlo and Georgia O'Keeffe, as well as lesser-known but equally impressive women such as Disneyland's It's a Small World designer Mary Blair, sculptor and Japanese-American internment survivor Ruth Asawa, and children's book illustrator Alice Provensen, who at ninety-seven is our longest-living lady featured here.

All of the women included in this book had to overcome significant obstacles in society and their personal lives in order to pursue their dreams and realize their artistic ambitions. One inspirational artist featured here that broke from convention was Sister Mary Corita Kent. Sister Corita was part of the progressive order of nuns at Immaculate Heart in Los Angeles during the 1960s. Sister Corita not only taught art but created hundreds of original, colorful, and graphically bold silkscreened works that often incorporated clever references to advertising as well as spirituality. She was dedicated to the ideals of helping the poor and underserved, and to uplifting the values and desires of a just society through her artistic messages of love and peace. In one of her pieces from 1969 she depicted Martin Luther King Jr. with her signature handwritten text that reads, "The King is dead. Love your brother." Eventually, the Immaculate Heart nuns were deemed too radical for the archdiocese in their quest for modest changes and self-governance, ultimately resulting in their decision to leave the Catholic Church altogether. Luckily, Corita Kent continued to paint her optimistic and beautiful hopes for humanity until the end of her life.

Artist Yayoi Kusama has lived an eccentric life of devotion, one might say obsession, to her work. Beginning in the 1950s through the 1960s, Yayoi Kusama began painting surfaces with her now-signature polka dots. These paintings, performance art pieces, and installations, including her amazing and immersive *Infinity Mirrored* rooms, were all manifestations of the hallucinations she has experienced for most of her life. In fact, since the 1970s, Yayoi Kusama has voluntarily lived in a mental hospital in Japan a short distance away from her studio. Despite this unusual setup, or more likely because of it, Yayoi Kusama has emerged as one of the most prolific and recognized artists of our time, with recent retrospective shows at both MoMA and the Whitney Museum of American Art in New York, as well as the Tate Modern in London. Now in her late eighties, Yayoi Kusama continues to create magic with her singular vision.

While some of the women featured here have had long, productive lives, others, like Eva Hesse, were tragically taken from us much too soon. In Eva's brief thirty-four years of life she suffered and survived through many seemingly insurmountable circumstances. Born to an observant Jewish family, as a young child Eva and her family escaped Nazi Germany and ultimately immigrated to New York. When Eva was ten years old, her mother committed suicide. Despite these traumatic events in her childhood, Eva Hesse went on to study art and received her undergraduate degree from Yale. She was a contemporary of minimalist artists Sol LeWitt and Donald Judd. But unlike the rigidity of much of these minimalist artists' works, Eva brought a handmade, organic, and almost sensual quality to her sculpture that emanated from her innovative use of materials. By experimenting using latex and fiberglass, Eva Hesse created series of slightly irregular yet repetitive forms in her compelling installations. In a career spanning just ten years before she sadly succumbed to cancer, Eva Hesse's soulful and ephemeral work continues to inspire artists to this day.

As difficult as it was during this time period for women artists in general, it was even more so for African-American women in the visual arts—all the more reason that Alma Thomas was so remarkable. Alma Thomas was born in the South, but her family relocated to Washington, D.C. to flee racial violence. As a girl growing up she had dreamed of becoming an architect, which was seemingly impossible at the time, but instead graduated from Howard University with a degree in fine arts. Alma Thomas went on to have a thirty-five-year career teaching art in junior high school. Upon her retirement in 1960, at the age of sixty, she embarked on her fine art career while the civil rights movement was still in its infancy. Influenced by Abstract Expressionism she created her own beautiful Color Field paintings, developing a bold, multi-hued, mosaic-like technique. In 1972, Alma Thomas became the first African-American female artist to have a solo exhibition at the Whitney Museum of American Art. Recently, President Obama and First Lady Michelle Obama proudly unveiled an Alma Thomas painting at the White House, the first artwork by an African-American woman to be featured there.

All of these women forged new territory in a day and age without many, if any, female role models in their given fields. It is a testament to their talent, enthusiasm, and determination that we luckily have them and their inspired work to look back on today. As artist Helen Frankenthaler said, "Go against the rules or ignore the rules. That is what invention is about." Here's to all of these rule-breaking and inventive women, and may they inspire the next generation of talented women to find their own artistic voices. Enjoy!

Gloria Fowler

New York, New York
October 28, 2015

Featuring

25

mid-century modern women

in the visual arts

Ray Eames

Edith Head

Peggy Moffitt

Yayoi Kusama

Frida Kahlo

Maija Isola

Sister Corita Kent

Coco Chanel

Bridget Riley

Ruth Asawa

Twiggy

Mary Quant

Louise Nevelson

Elaine Lustig Cohen

Helen Frankenthaler

Eva Zeisel

Georgia O'Keeffe

Florence Knoll

Edith Heath

Alma Thomas

Vera Neumann

Eva Hesse

Alice Provensen

Greta Magnusson-Grossman

Mary Blair

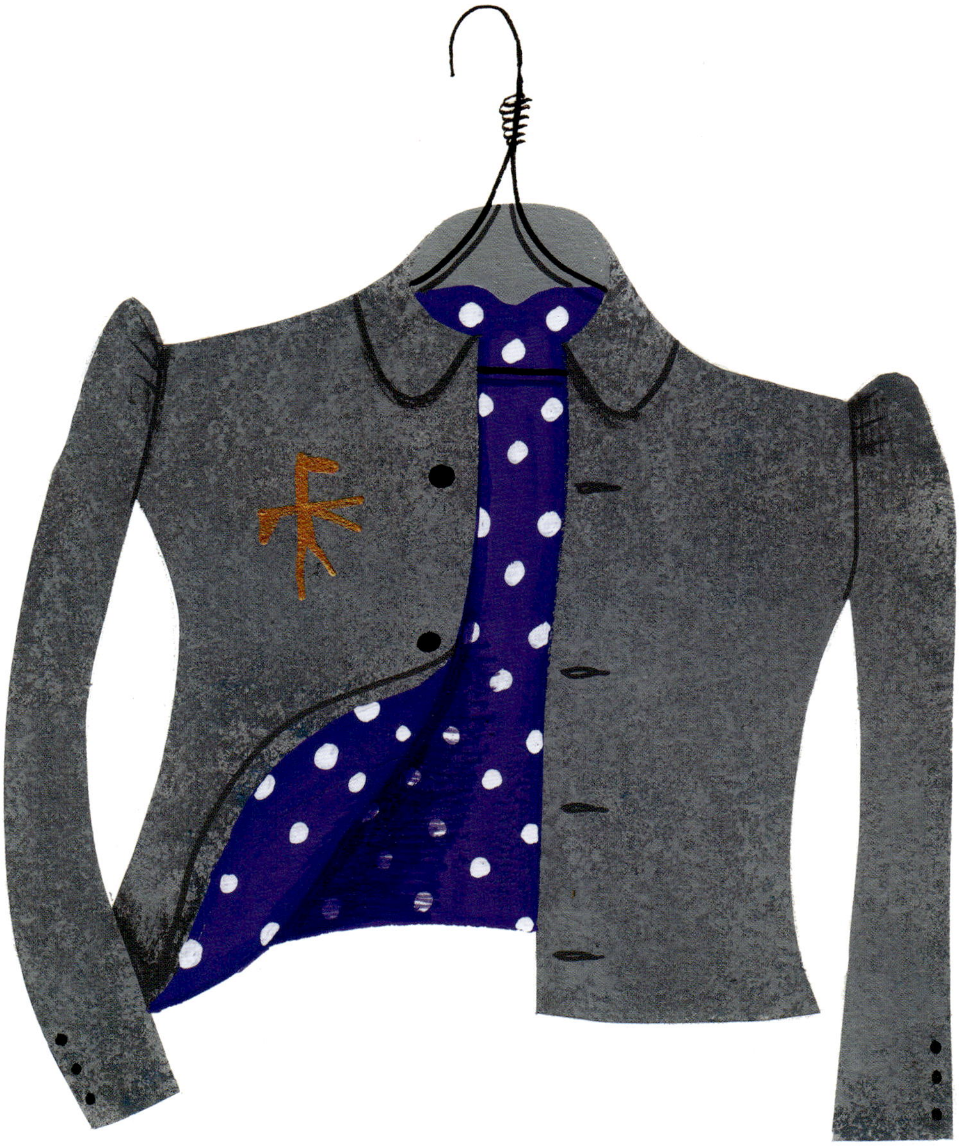

Ray Eames

“What works
good is better than
what looks good,
because what
works good lasts.”

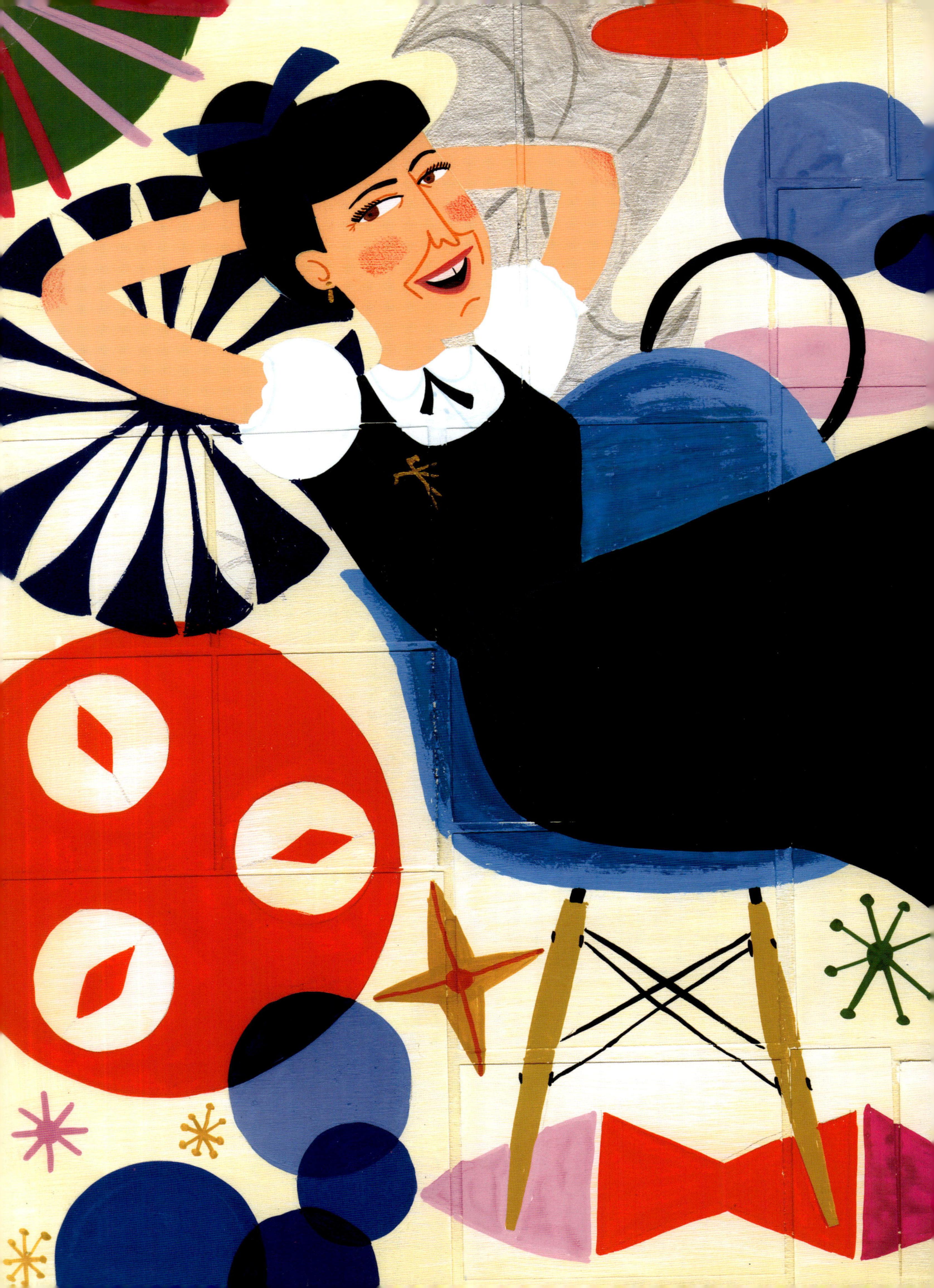

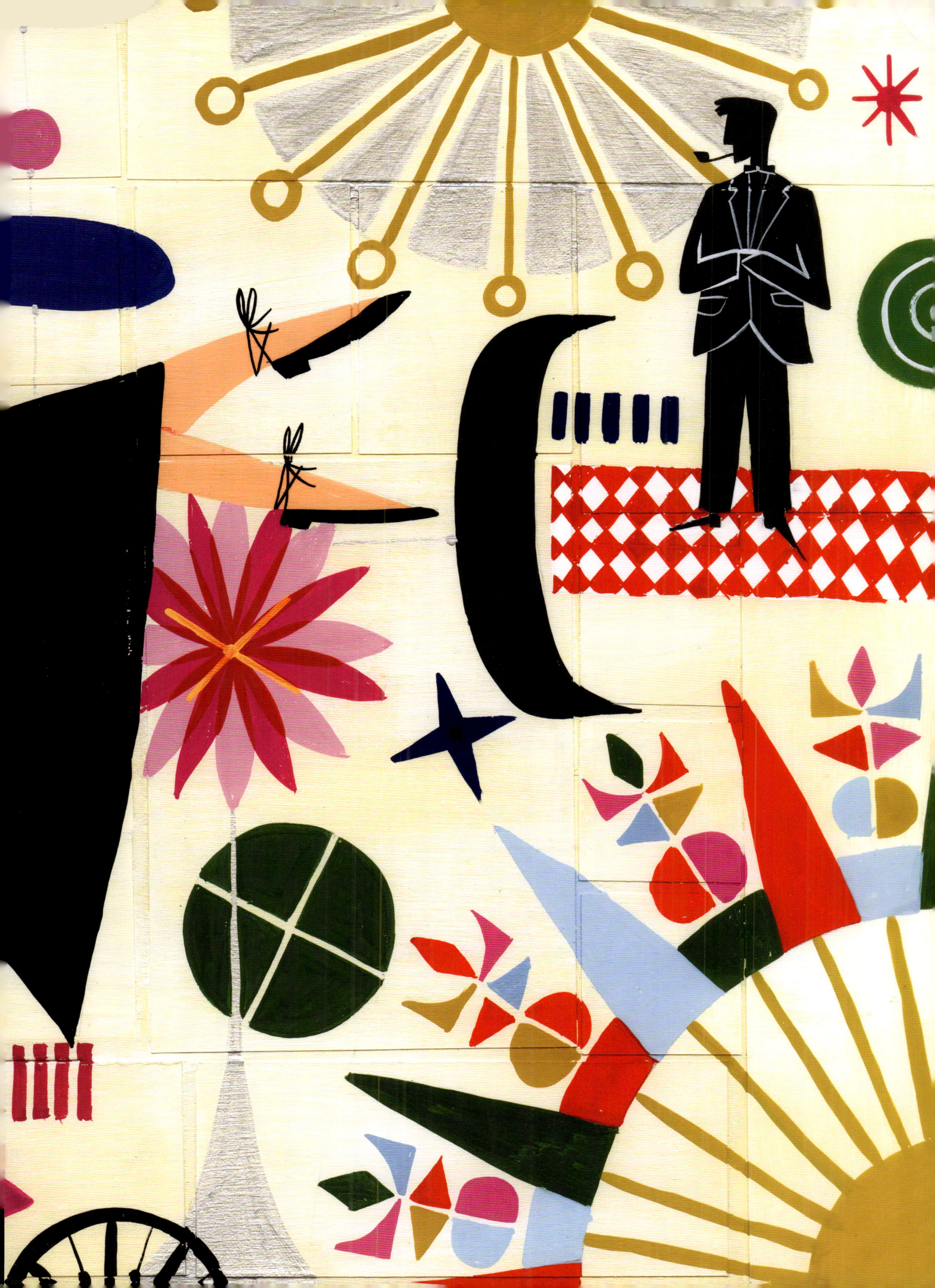

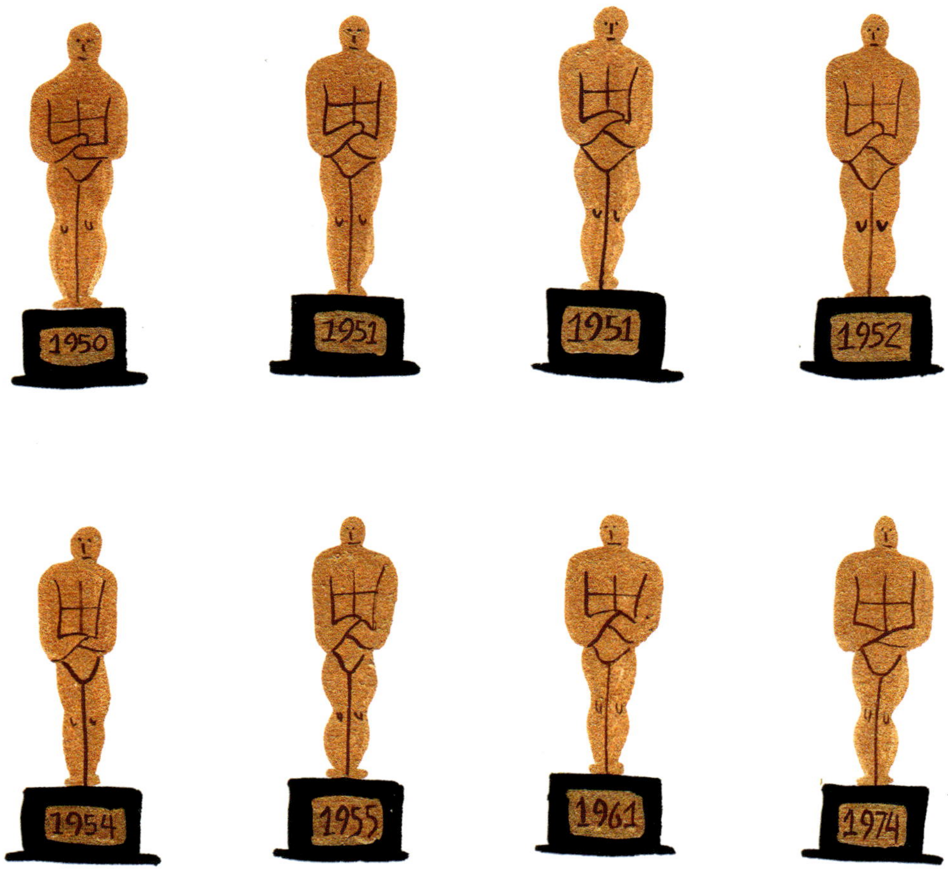

Edith Head

"You can lead a horse to water and you can even make it drink, but you can't make actresses wear what they don't want to wear."

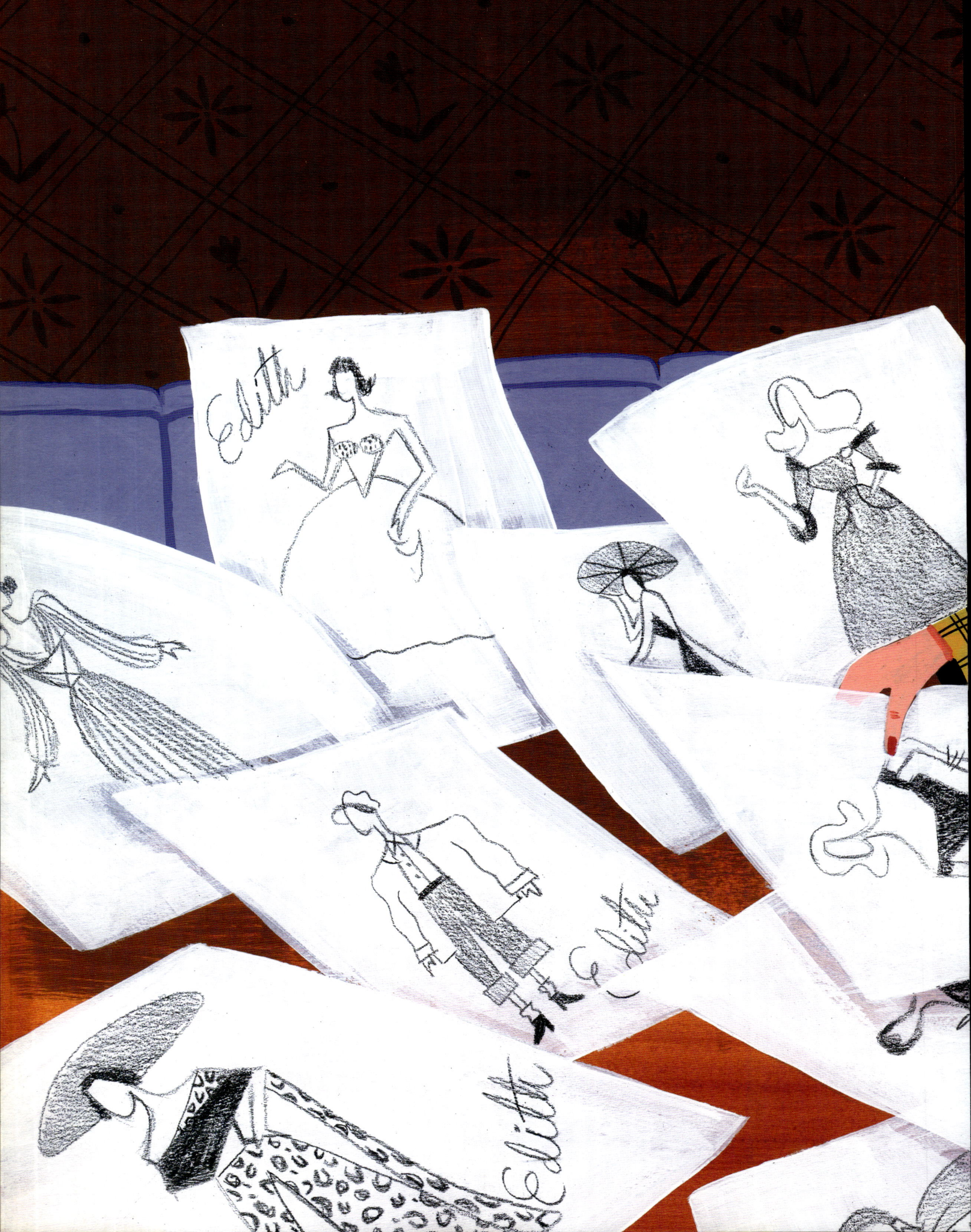
Edith
Edith
Edith

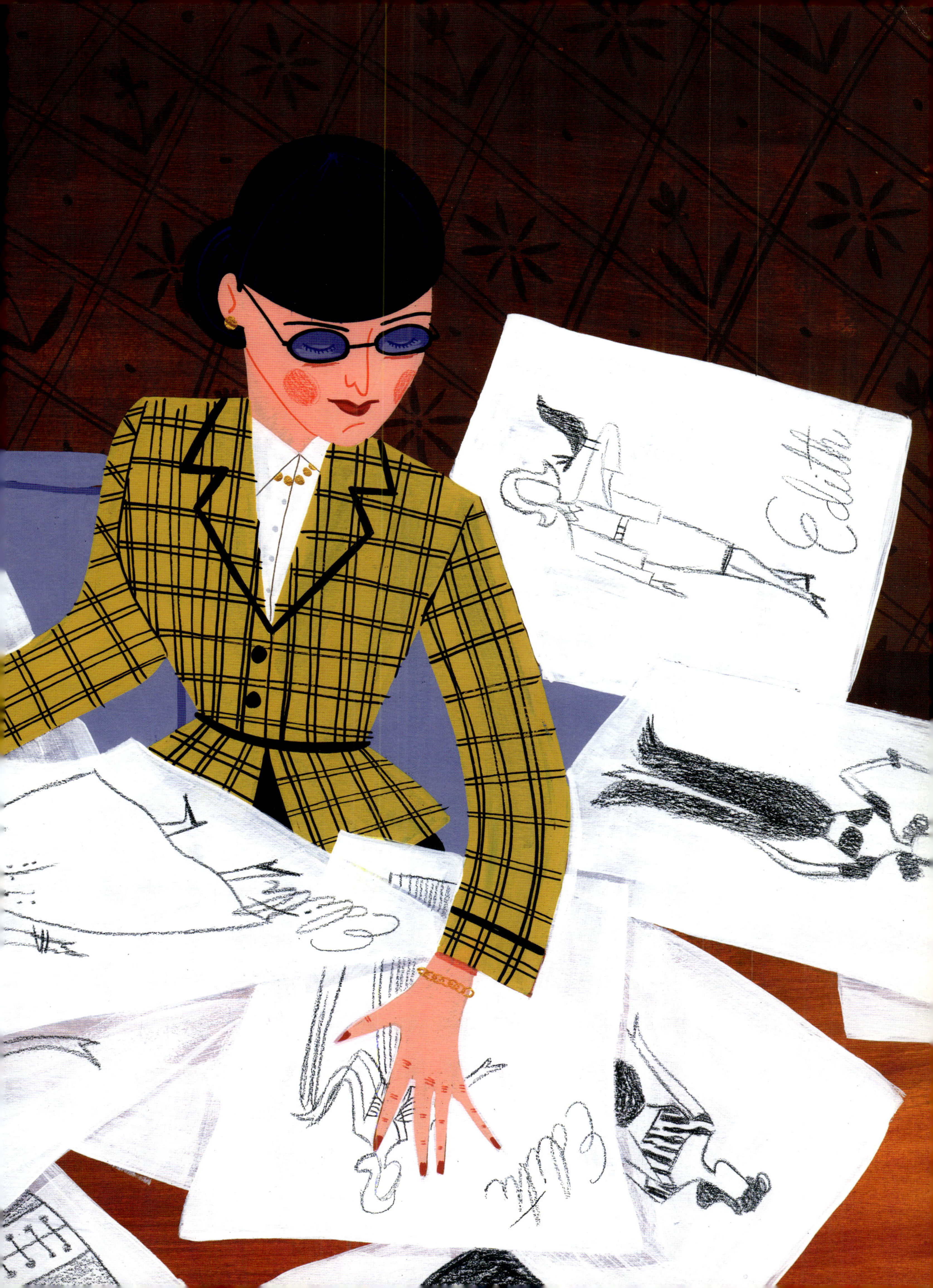
Edith

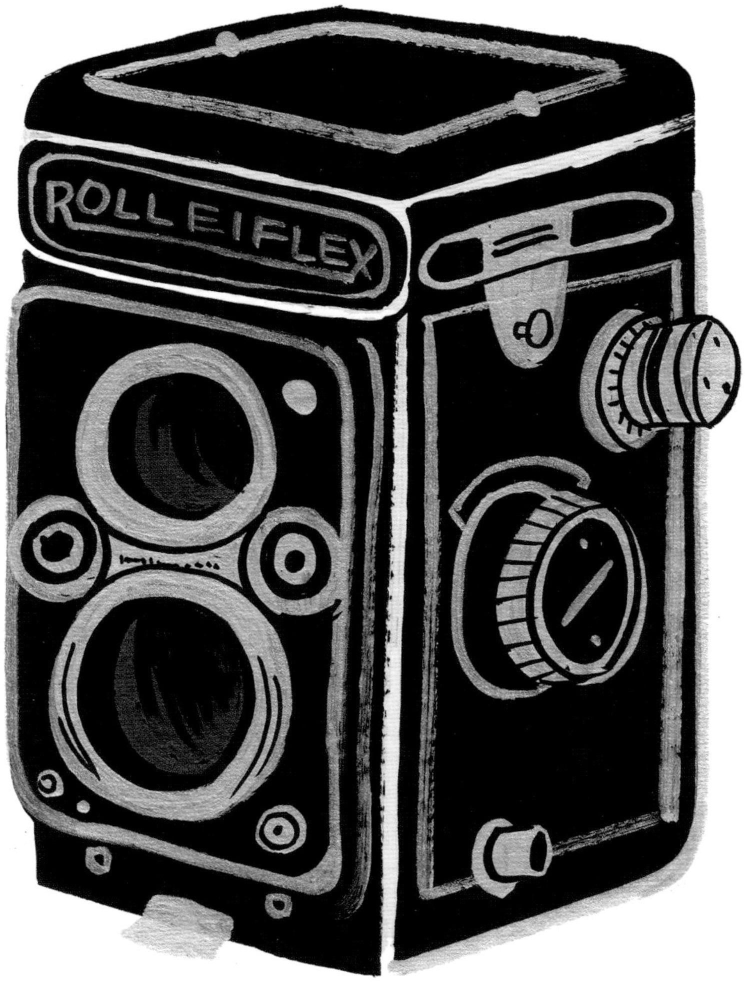

Peggy Moffitt

"I never held back. It was the height of freedom and liberation."

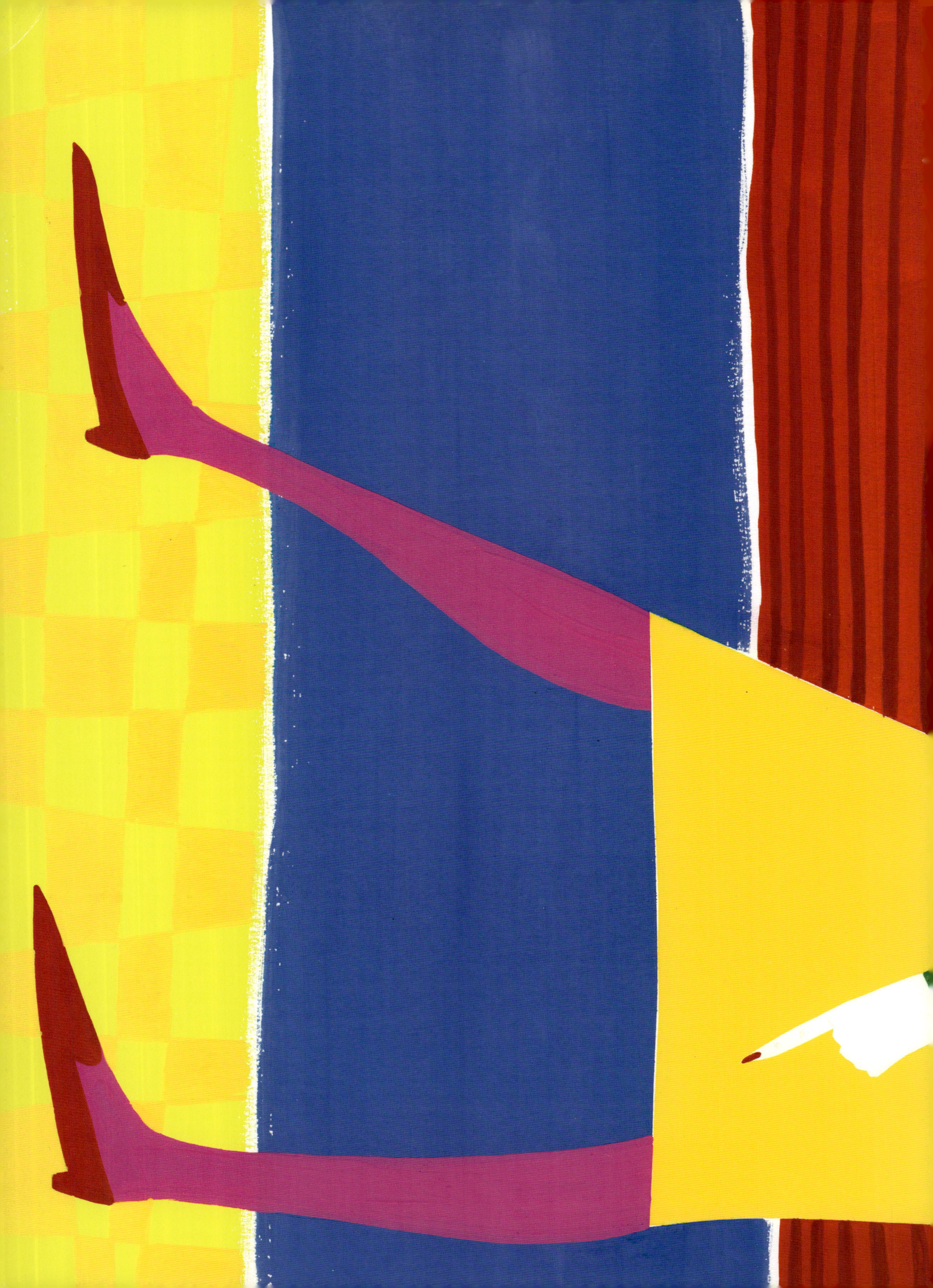

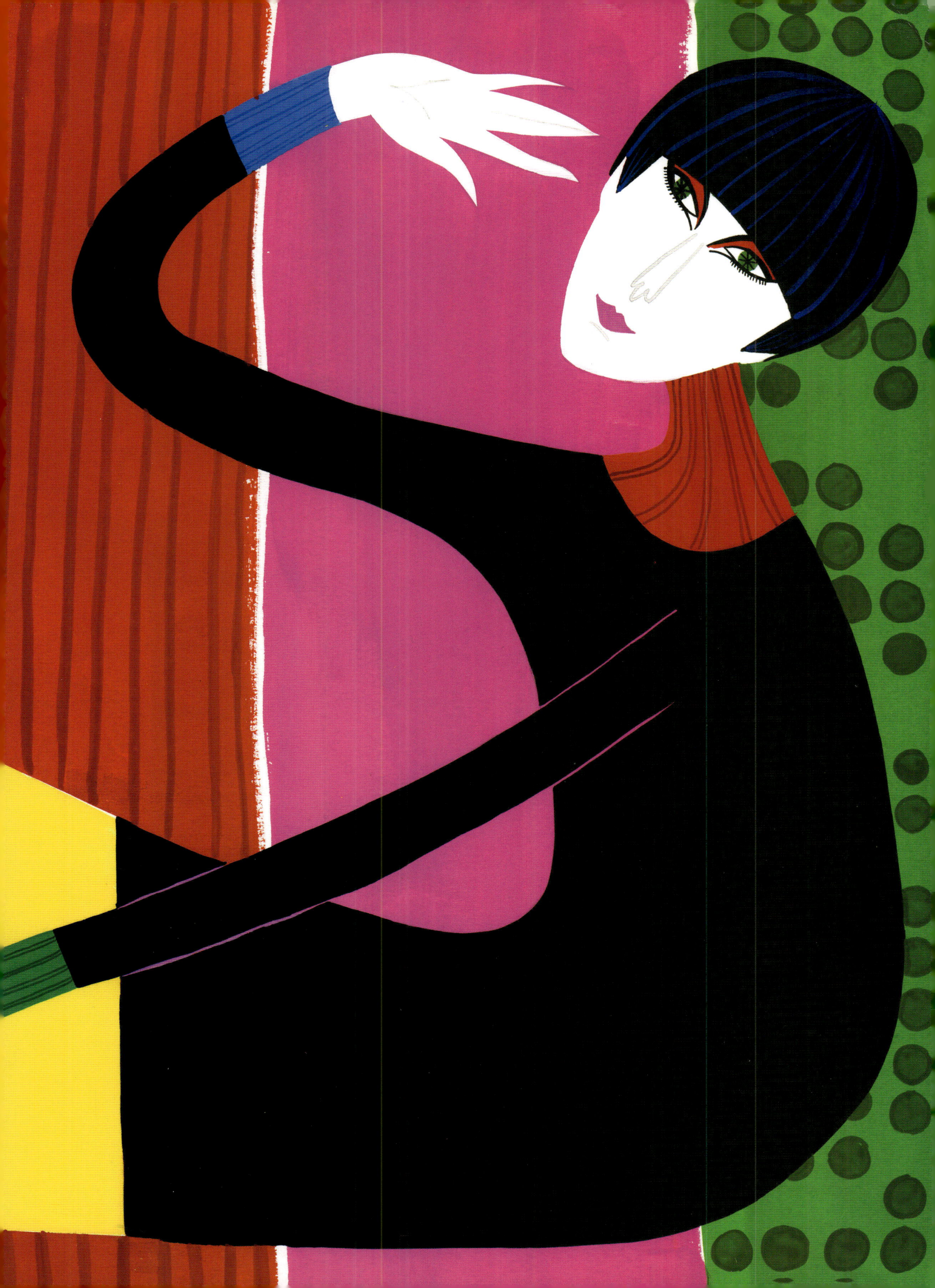

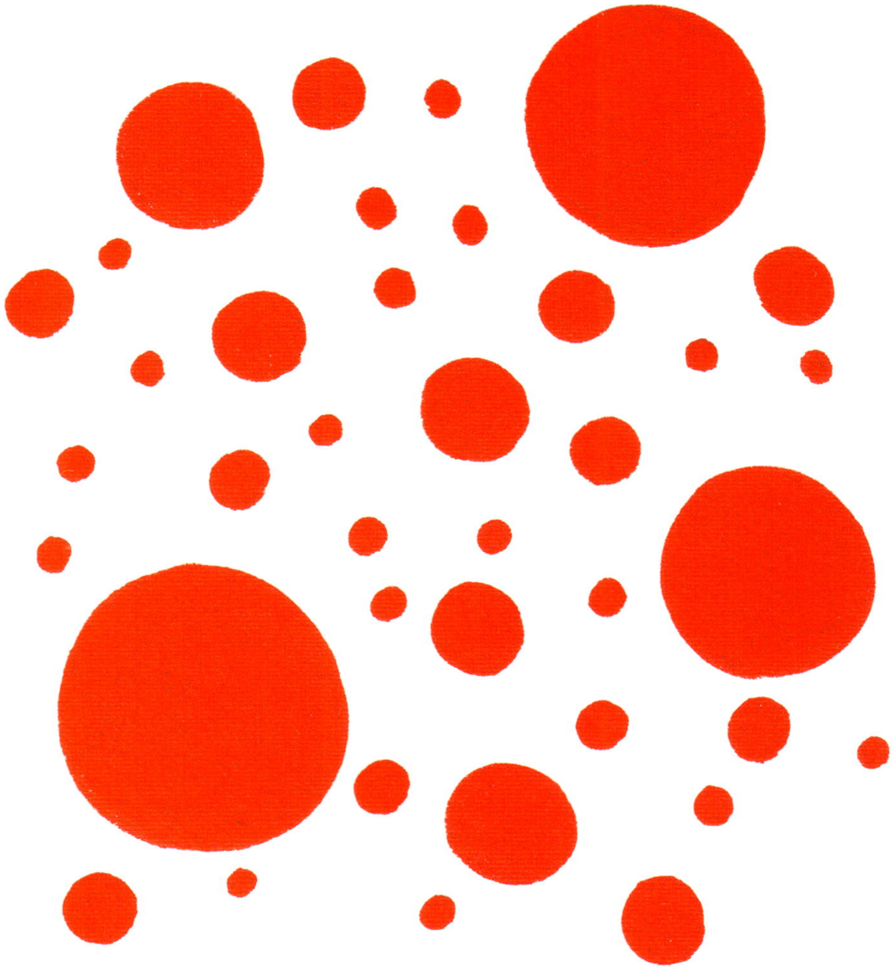

Yayoi Kusama

"Since my childhood, I have always made works with polka dots. Earth, moon, sun, and human beings all represent dots; a single particle among billions."

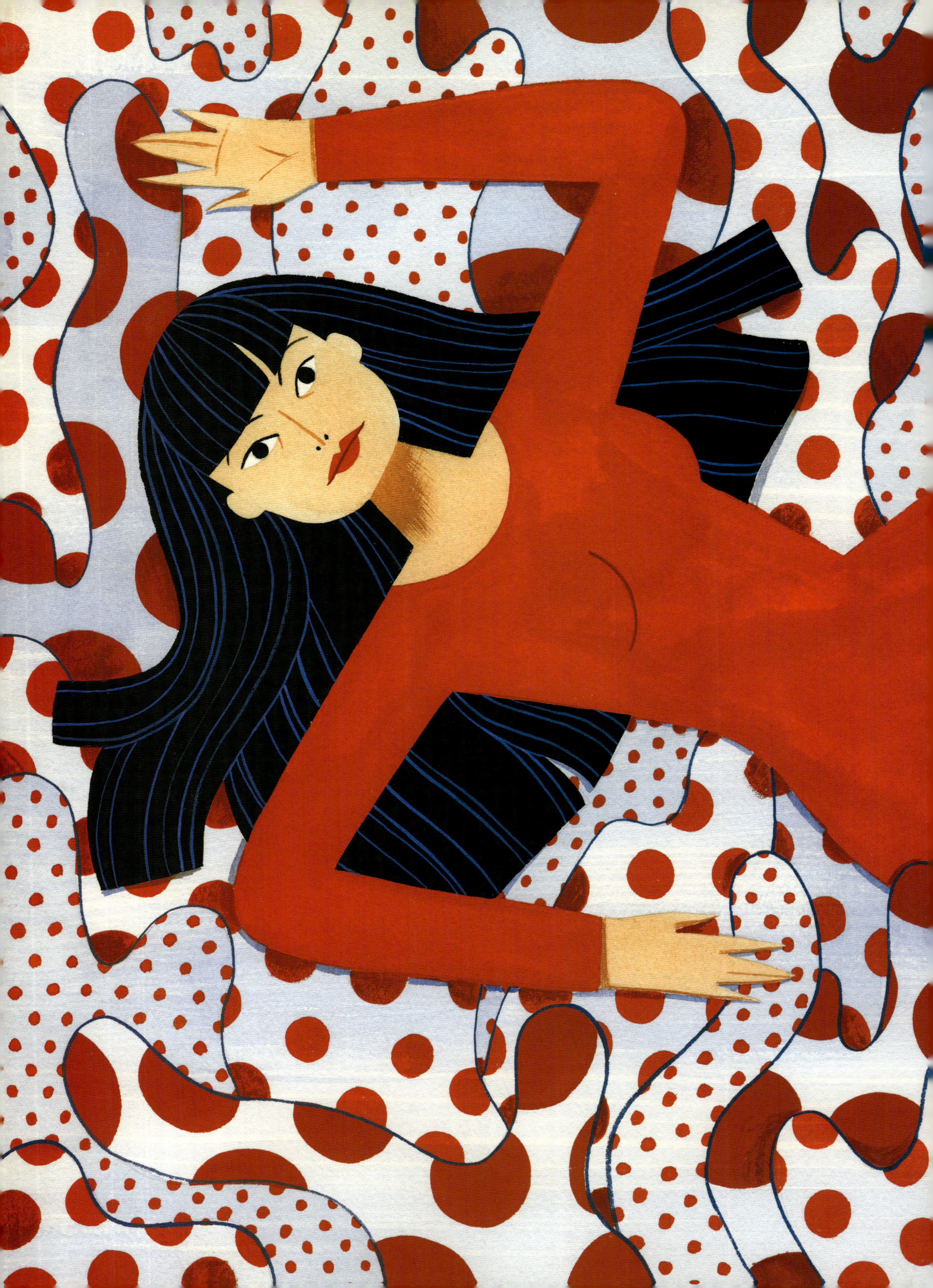

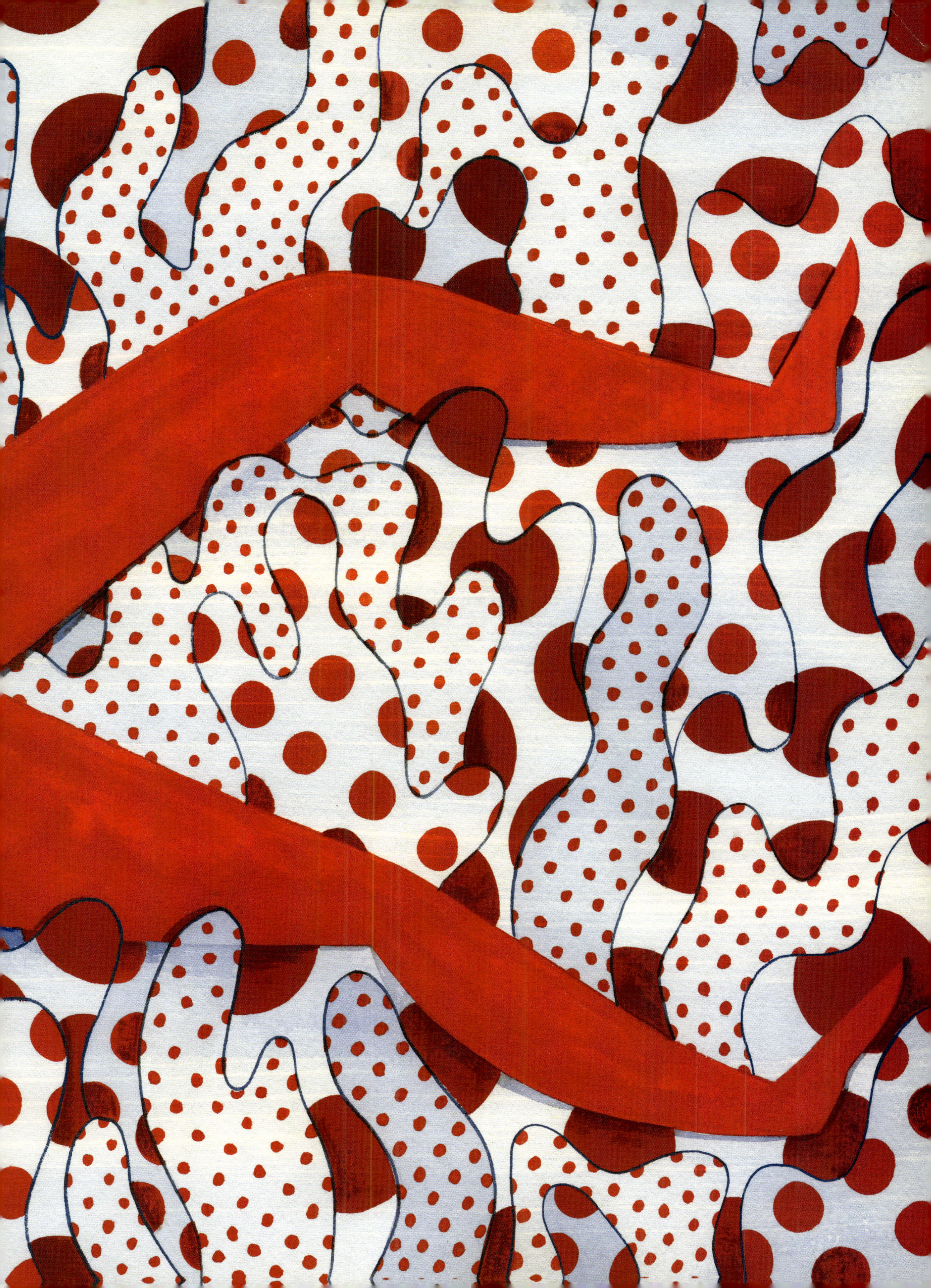

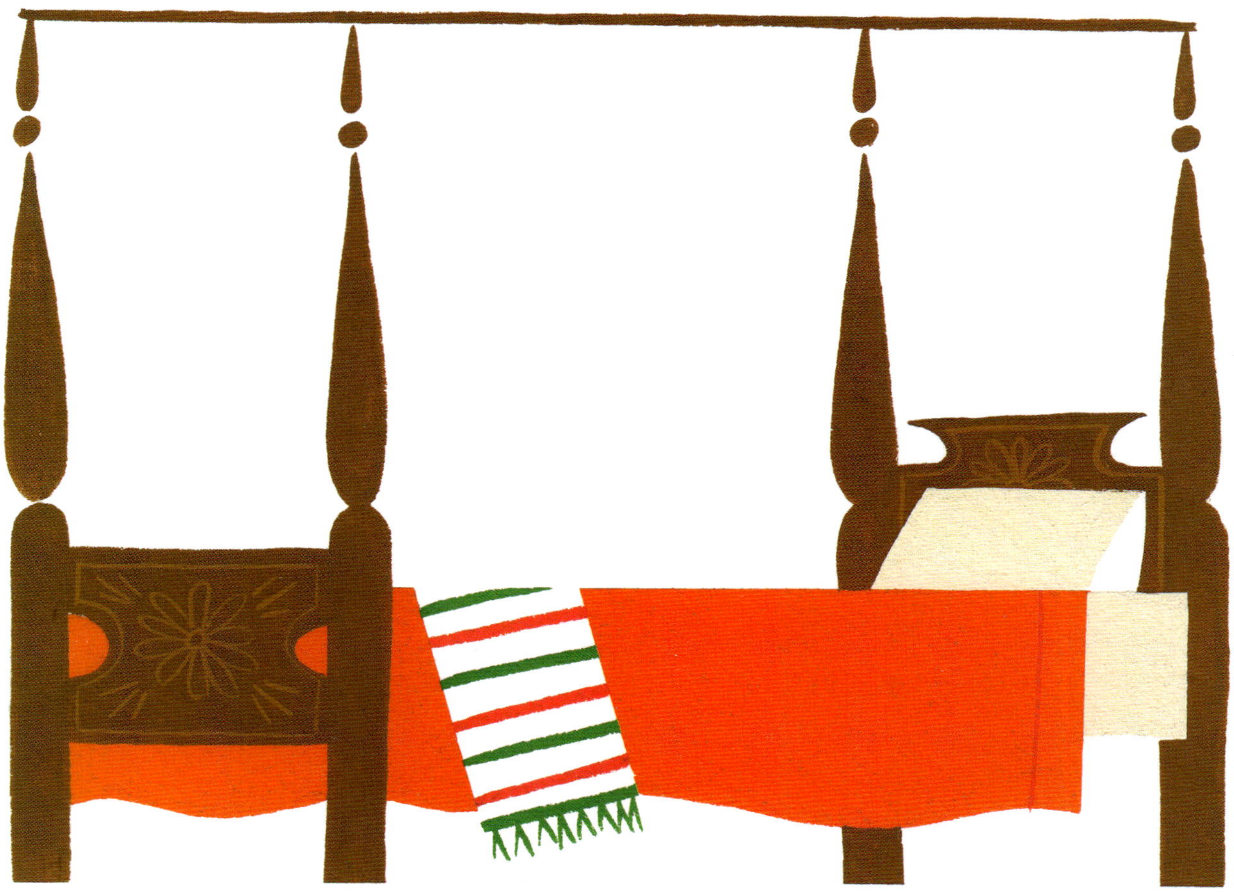

Frida Kahlo

"I never paint dreams or nightmares. I paint my own reality."

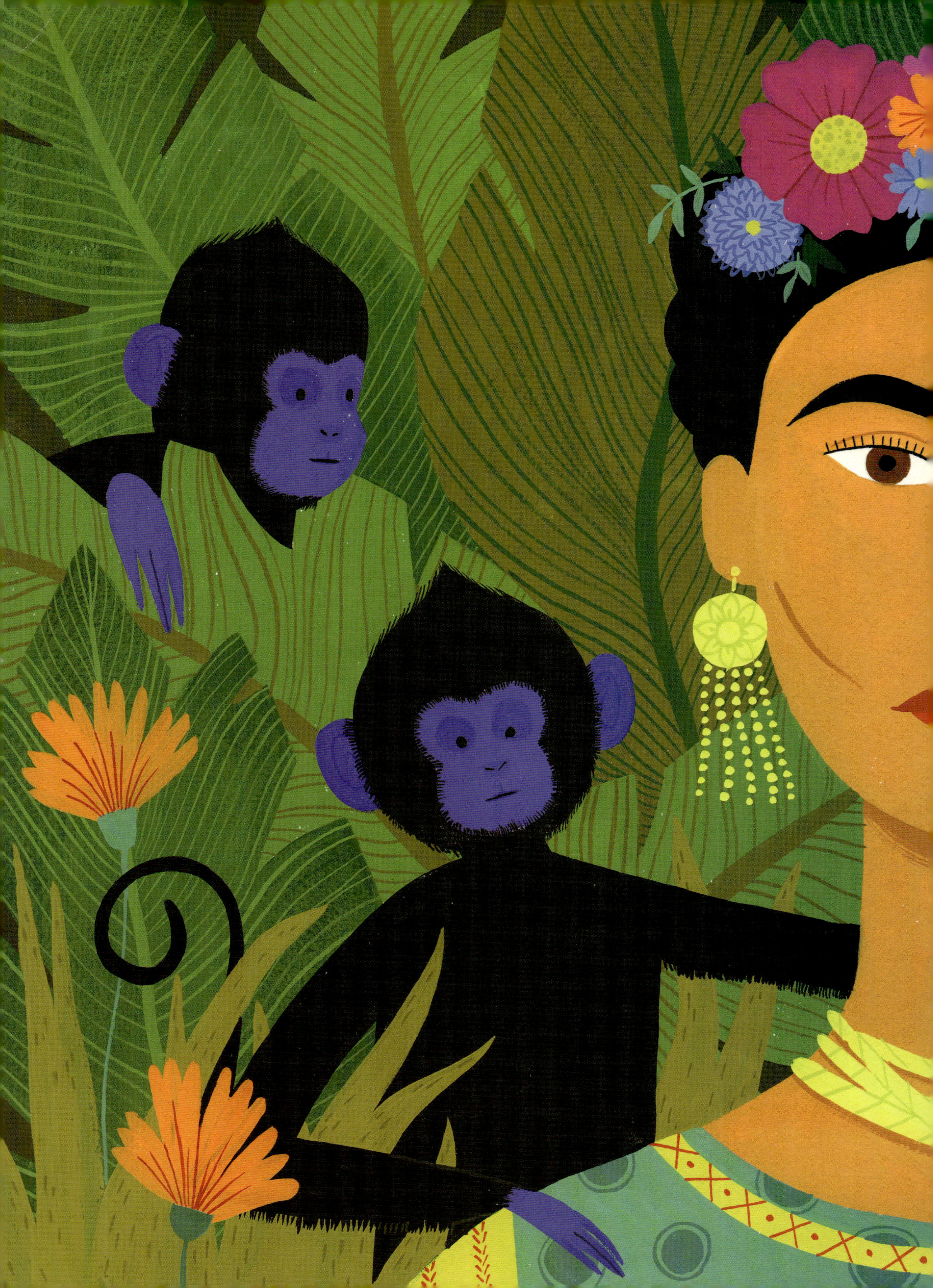

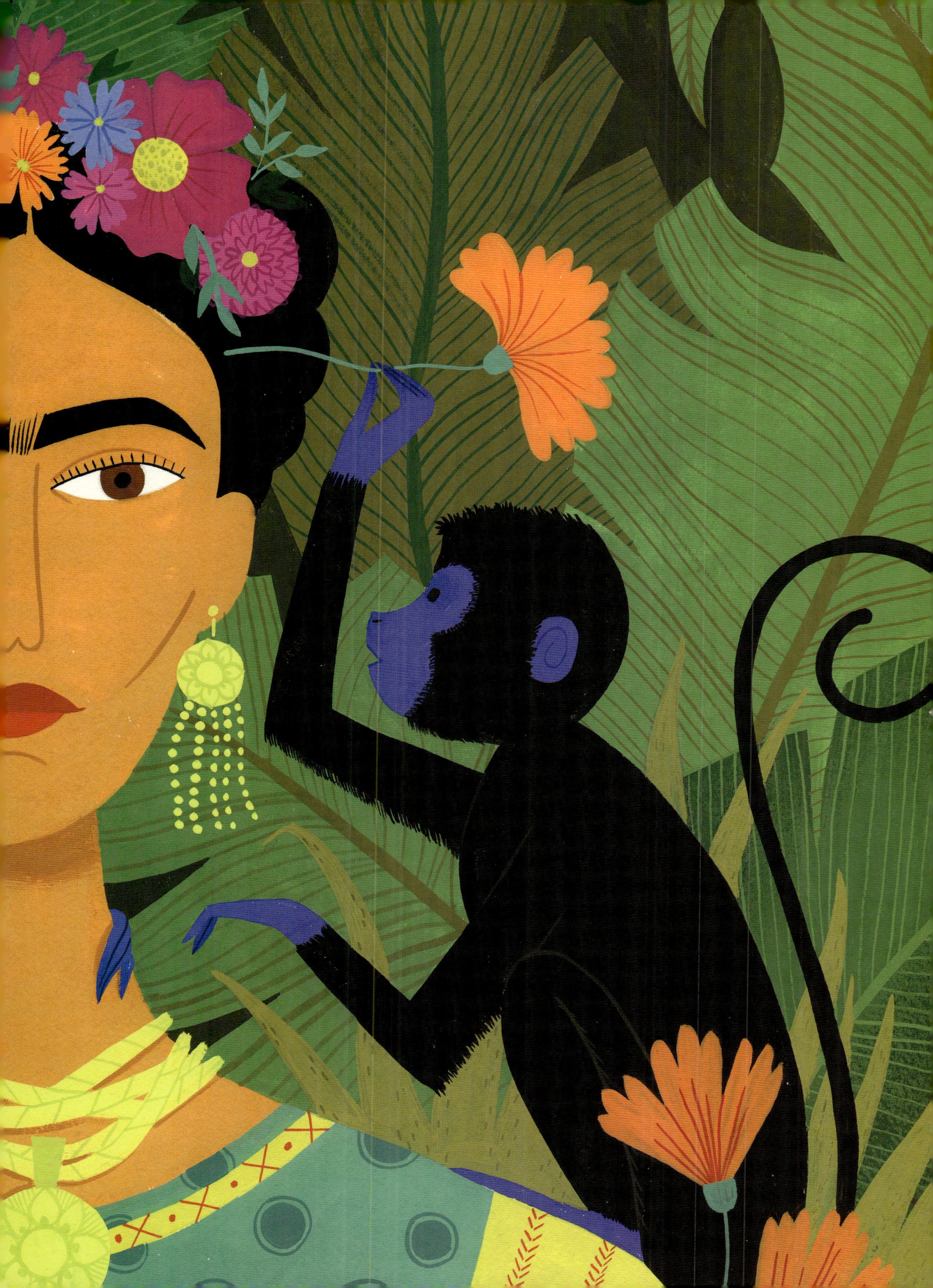

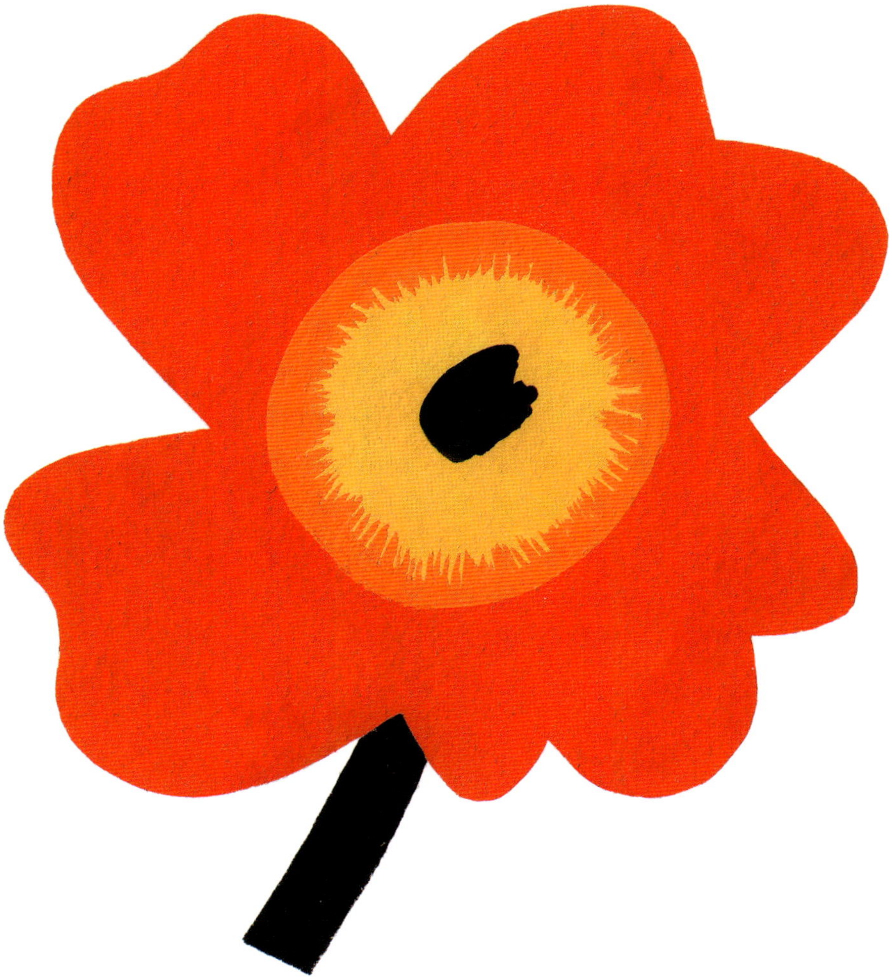

Maija Isola

“I tend to see everything in patterns … when I go see a film, look at snow and ice, wash dishes, or maybe the most when I am in love.”

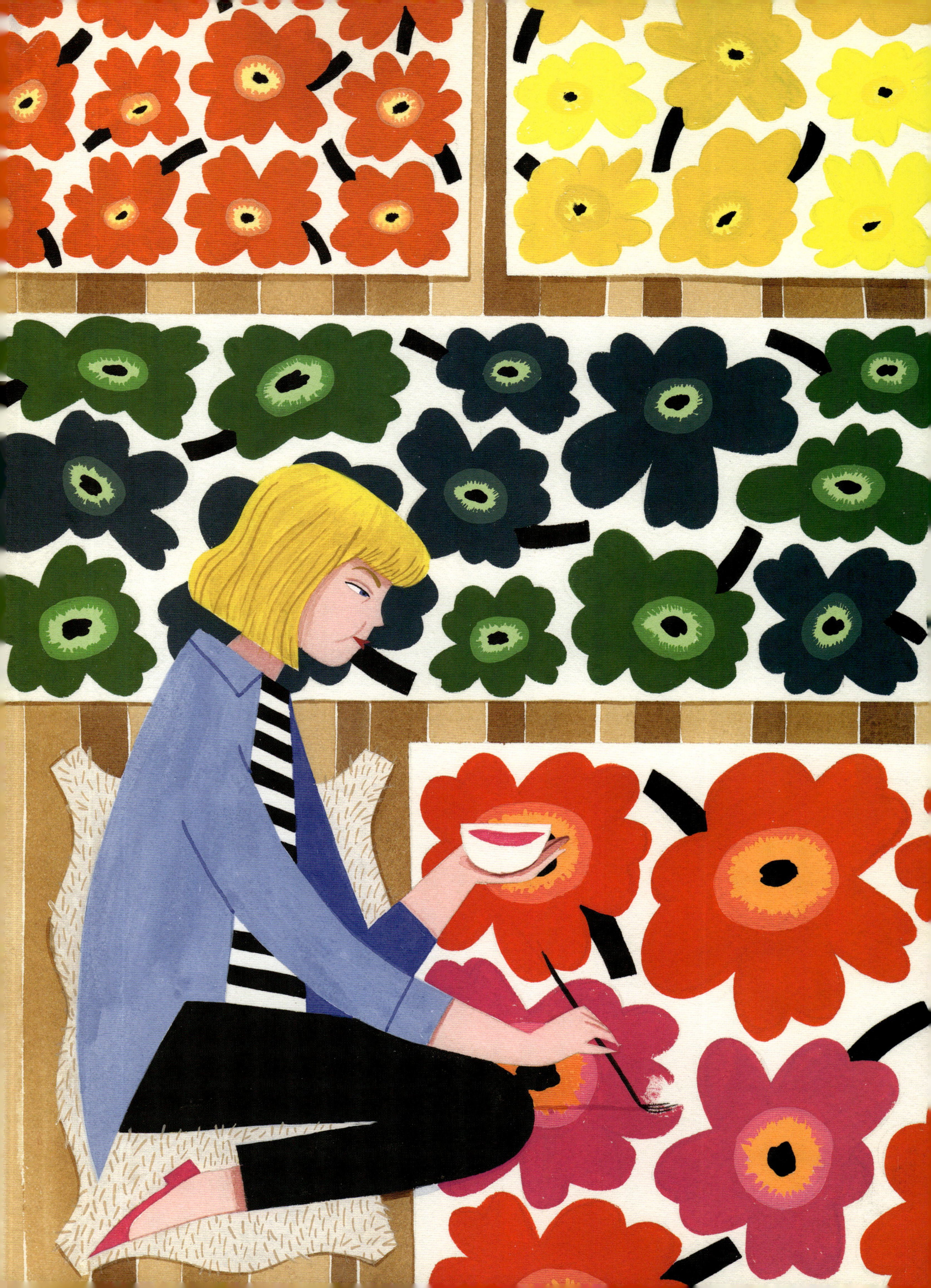

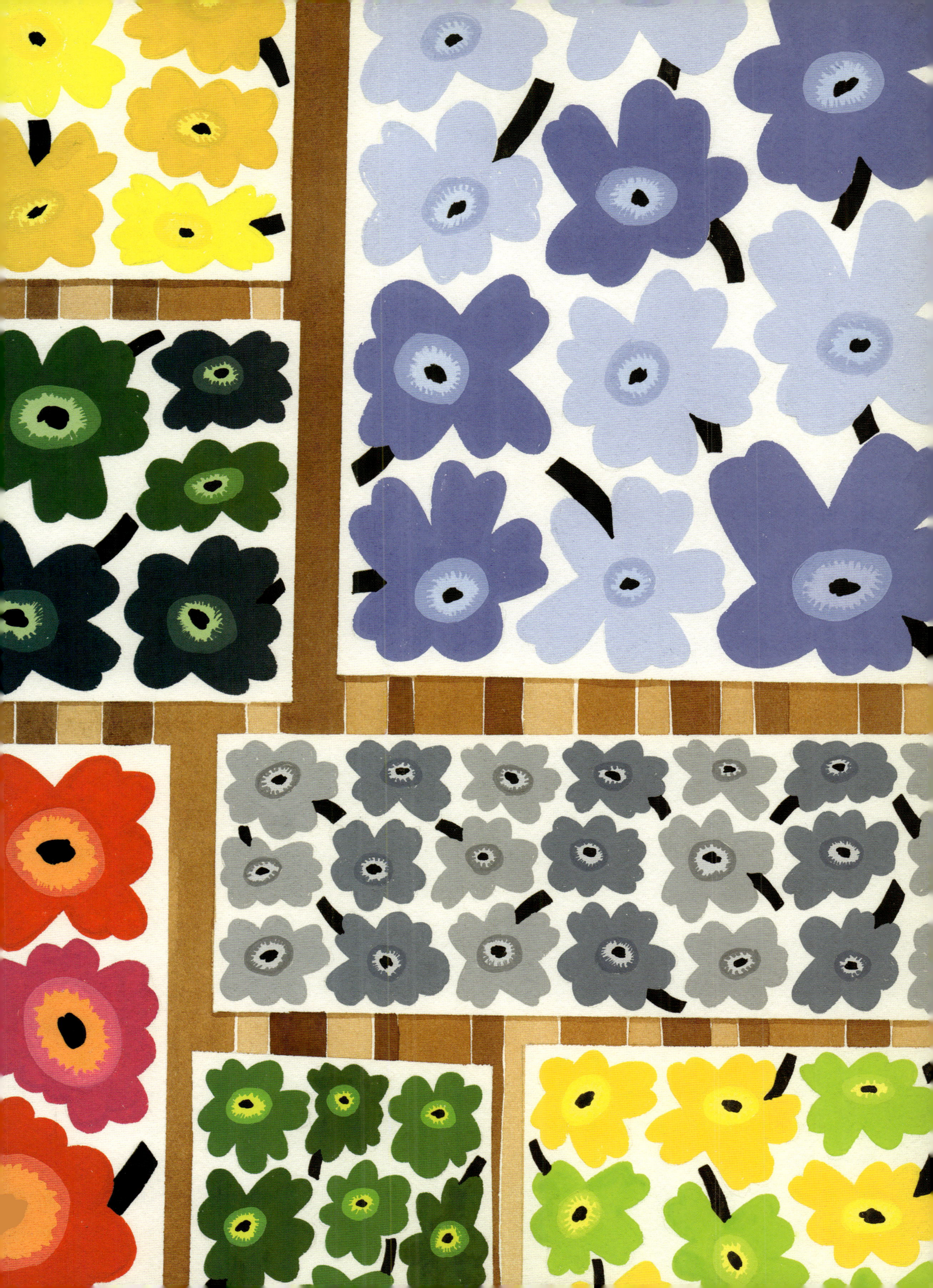

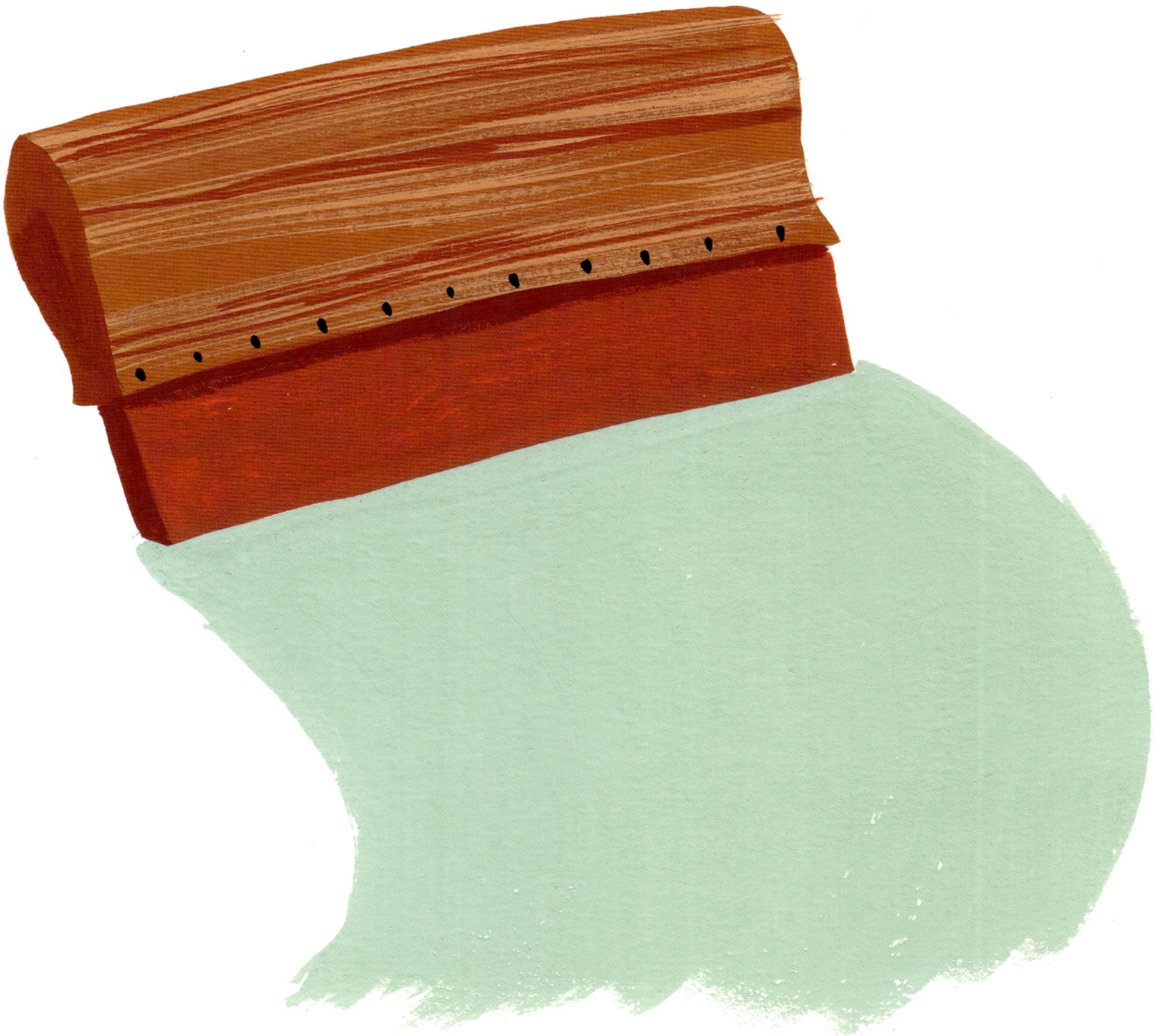

Sister Corita Kent

Rule 9:
Be happy whenever you can manage it. Enjoy yourself. It's lighter than you think."

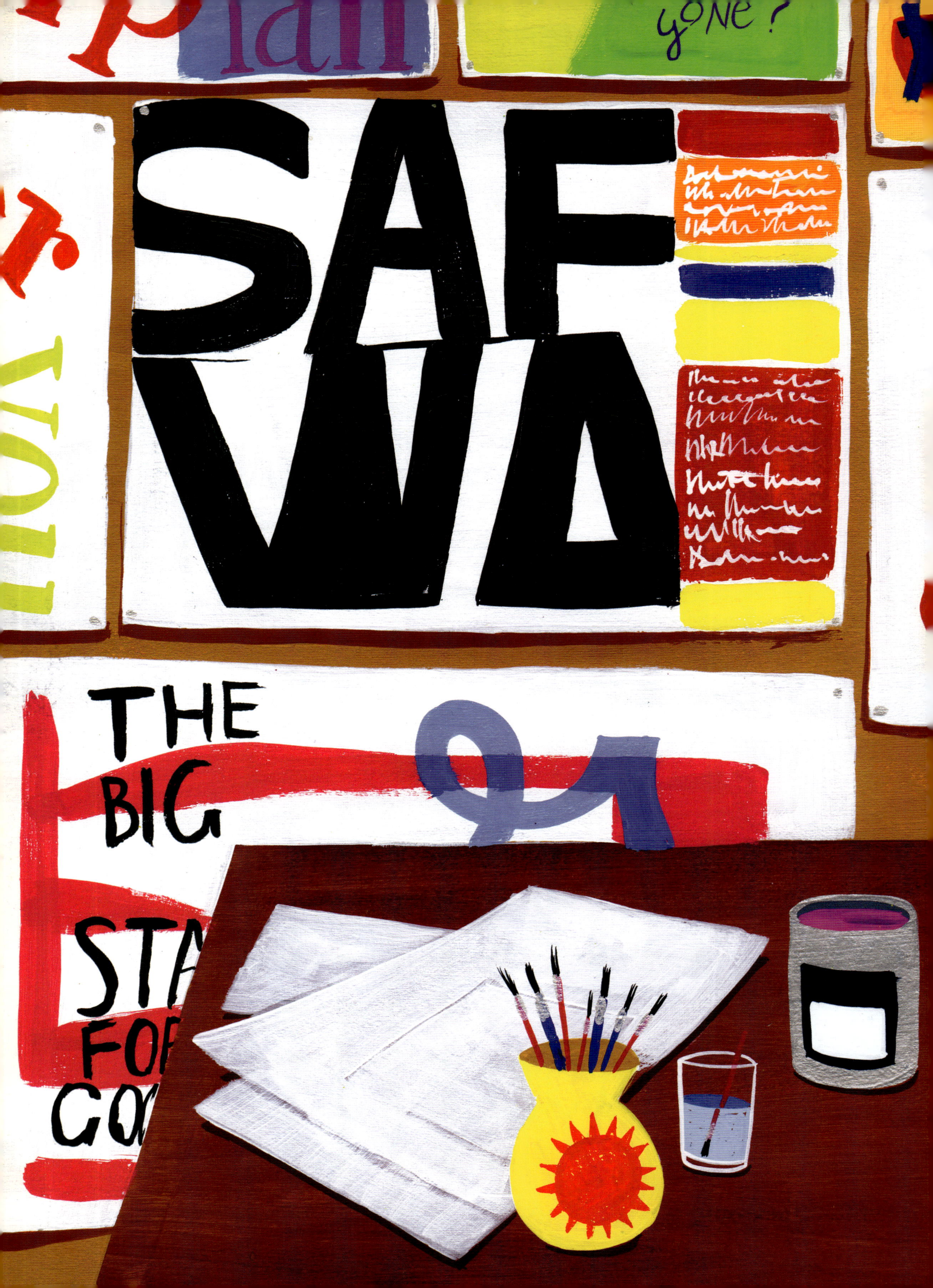
gone?
SAF
WA
THE
BIG

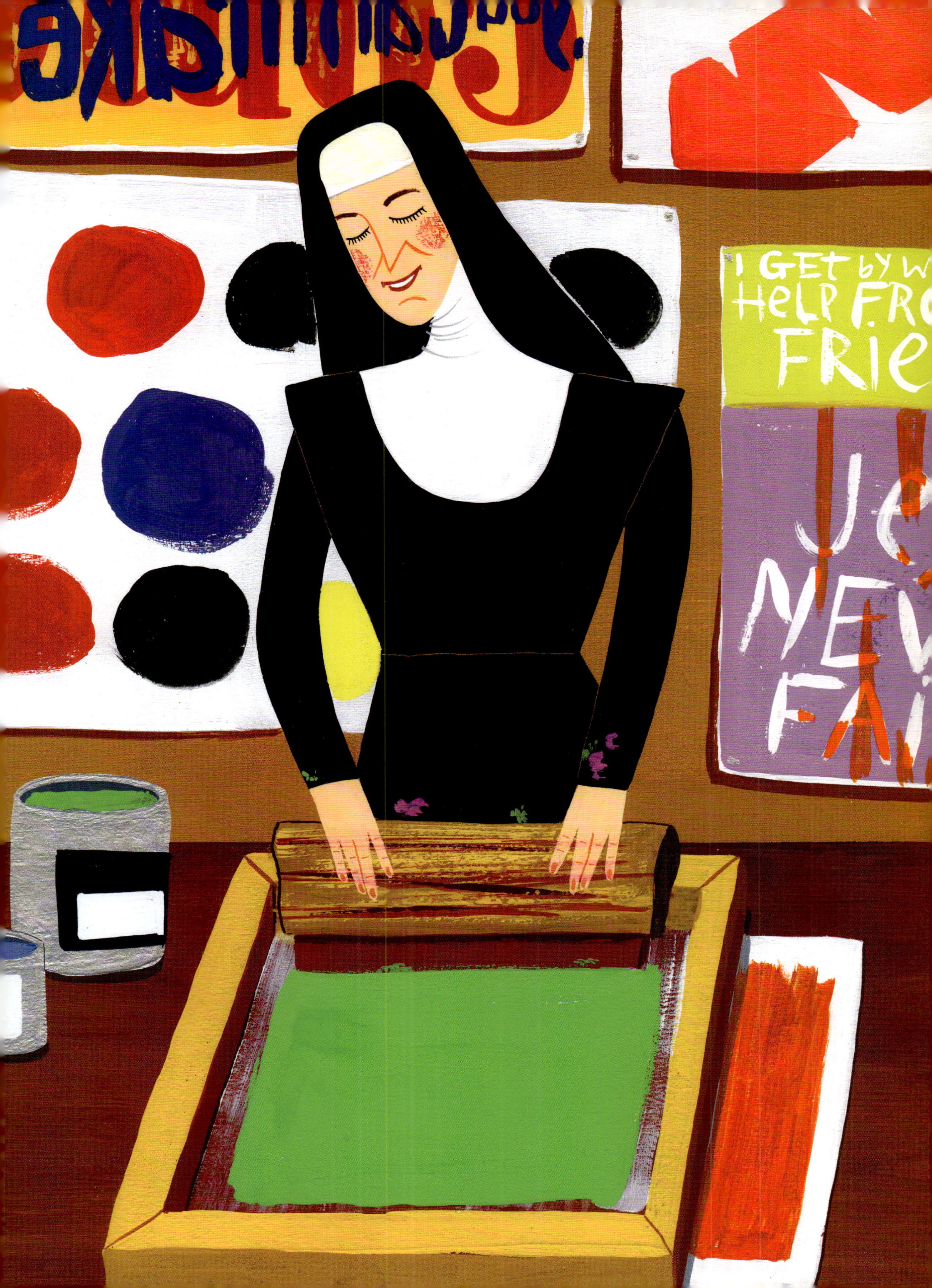

I GET by W
HelP FRO
FRIe
Je
NEV
FAI

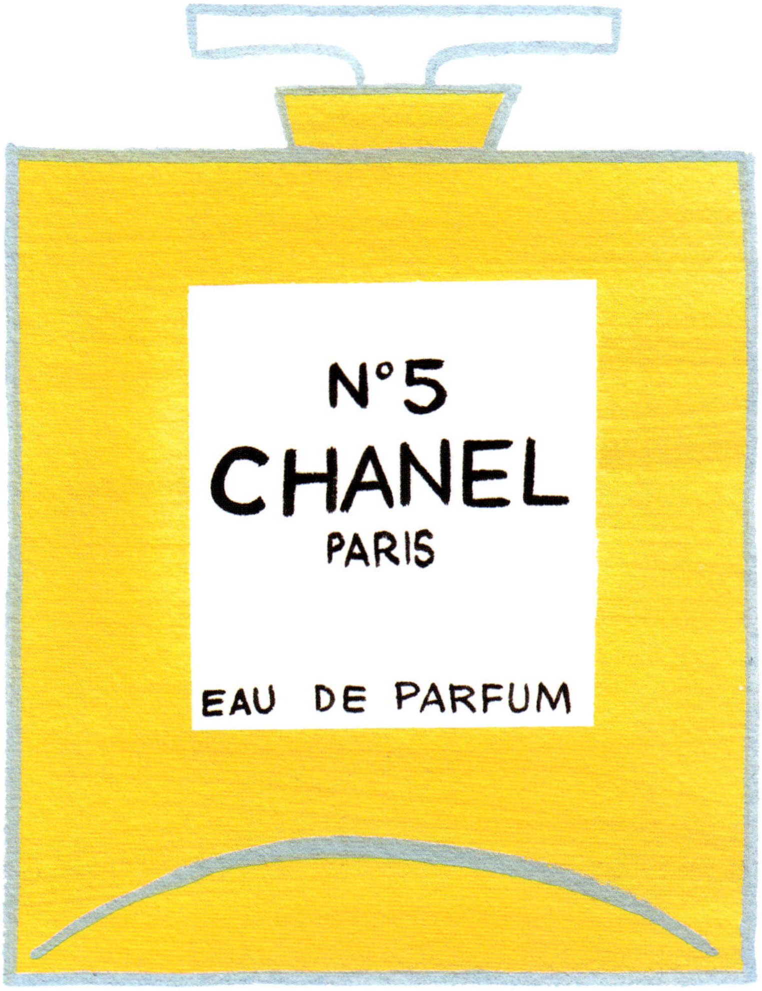

Coco Chanel

"A girl should be two things: classy and fabulous."

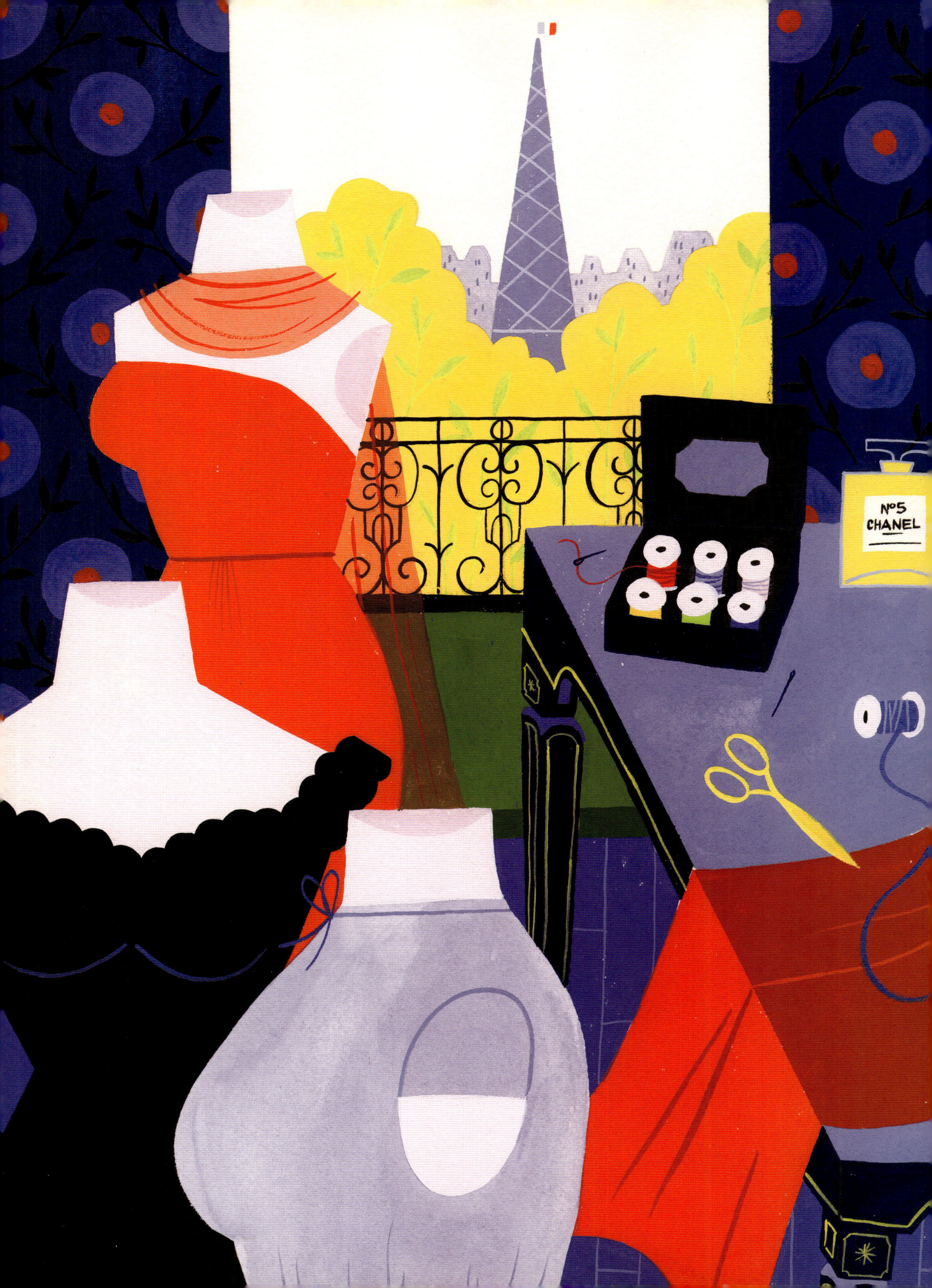
N°5
CHANEL

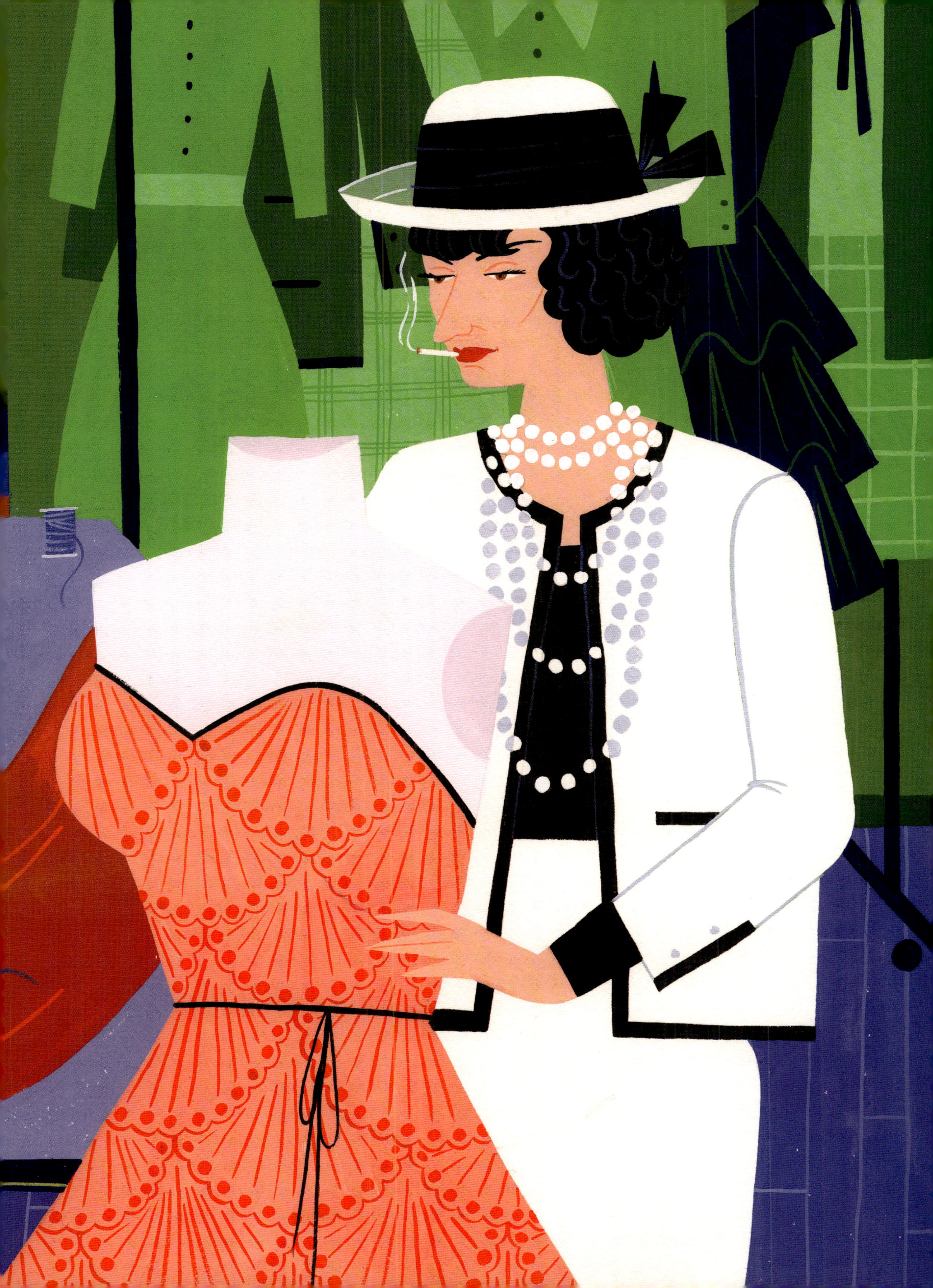

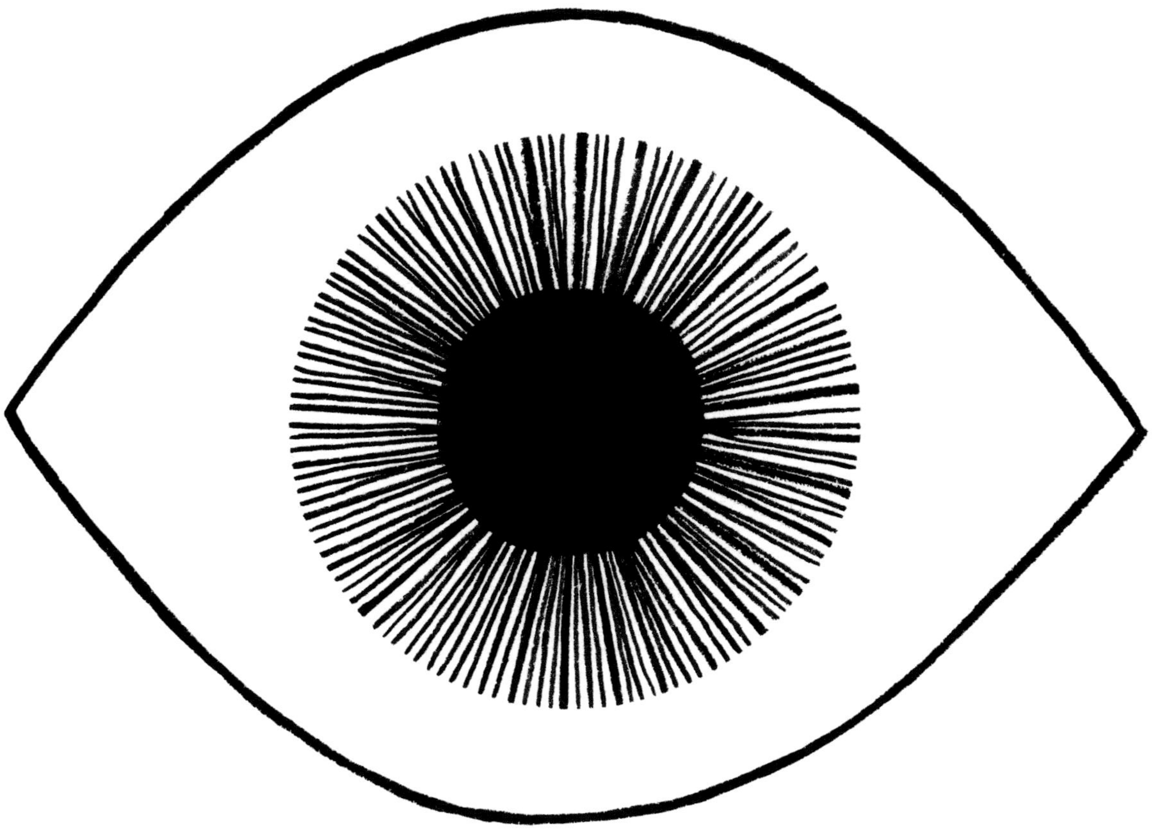

Bridget Riley

"Focusing isn't just an optical activity, it is also a mental one."

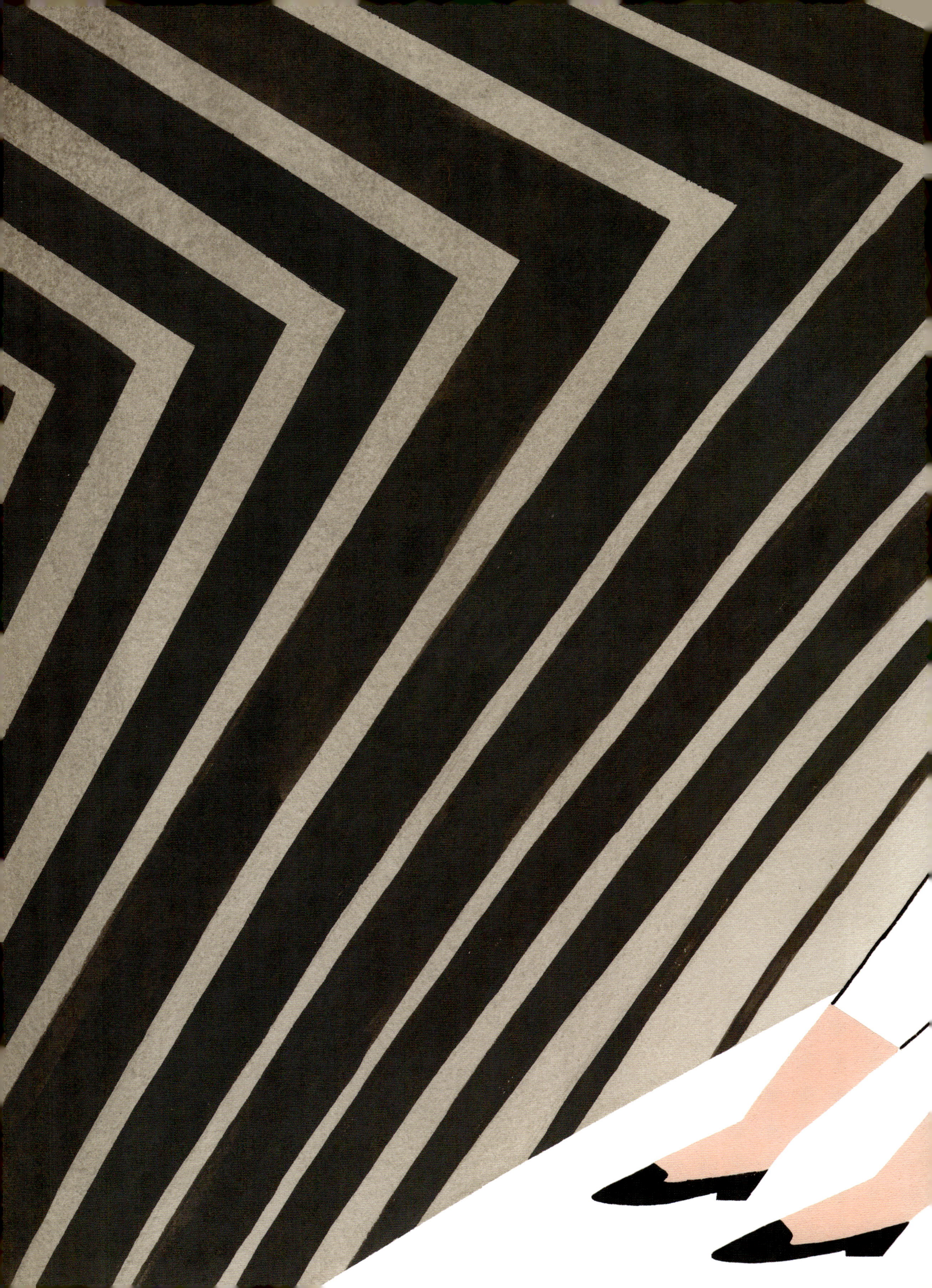

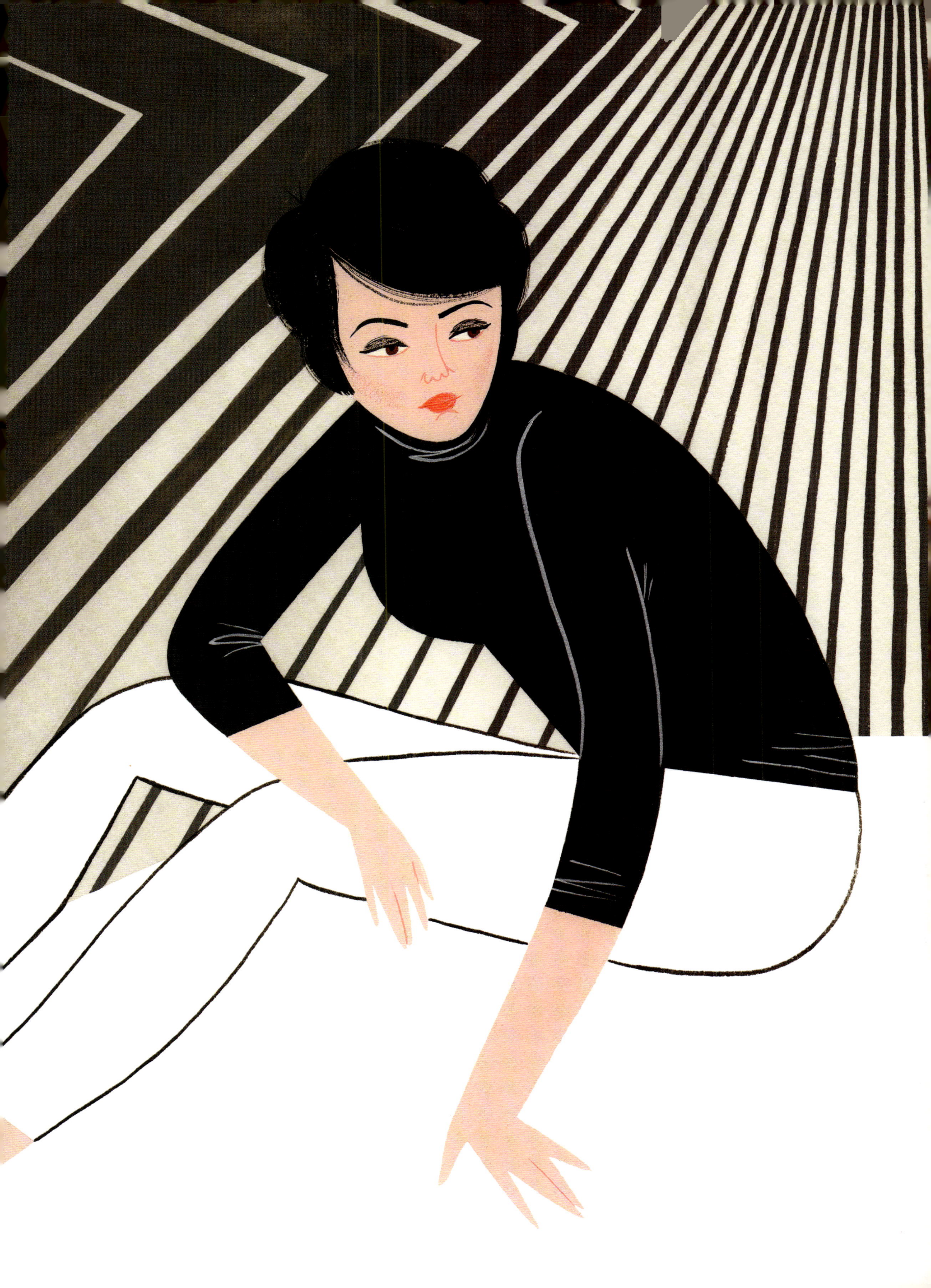

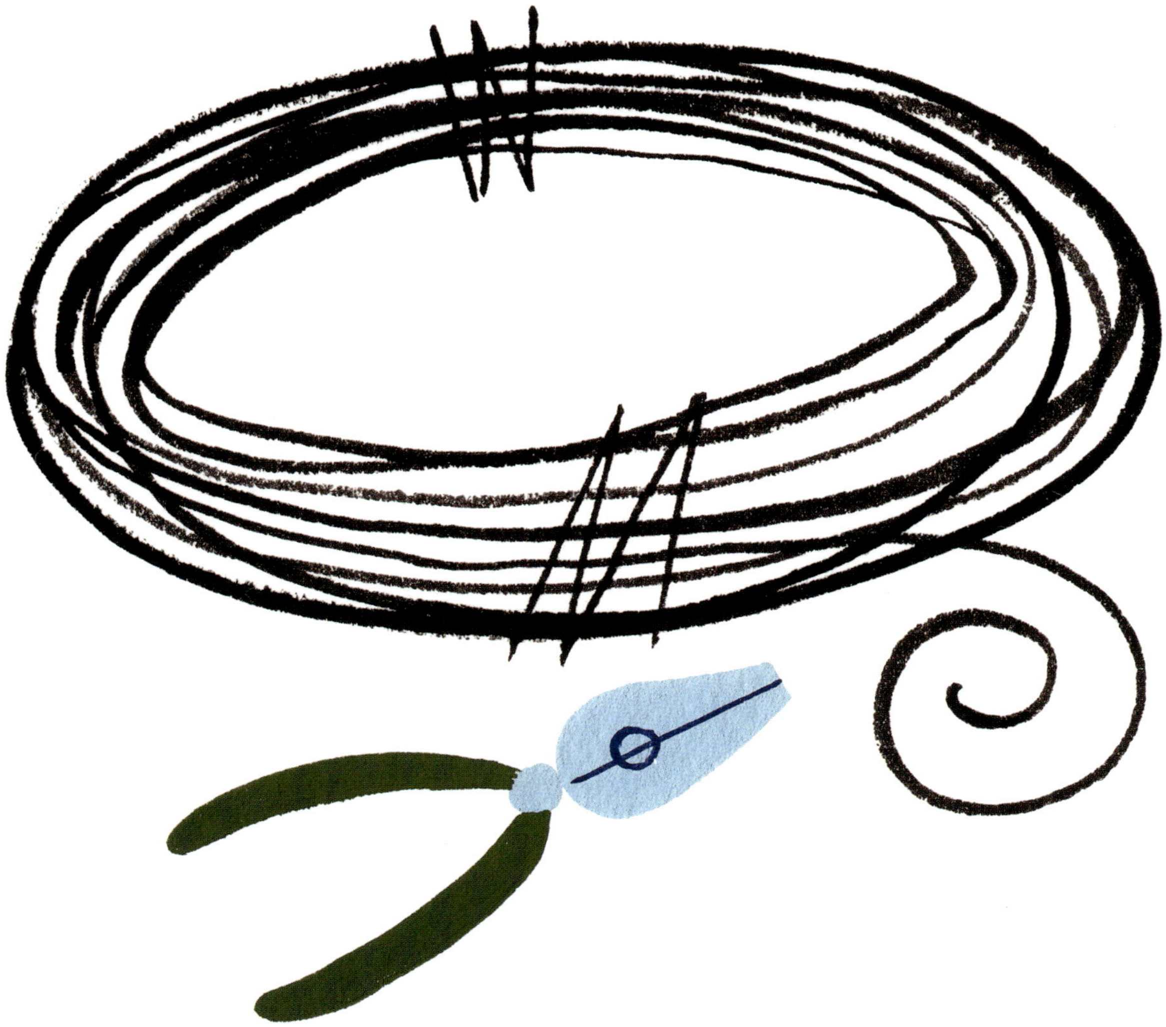

Ruth Asawa

“Sculpture is like farming. If you just keep at it, you can get quite a lot done.”

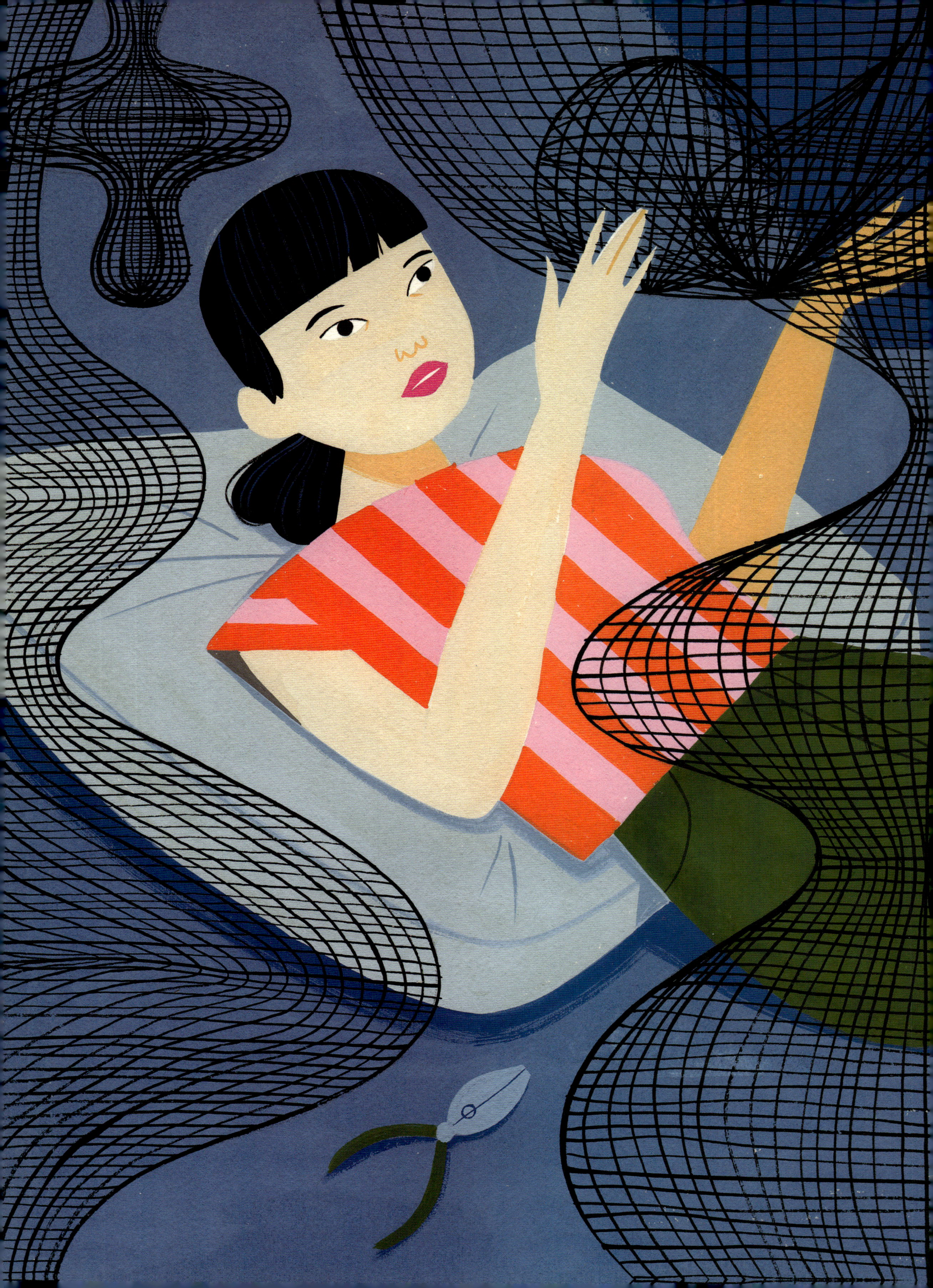

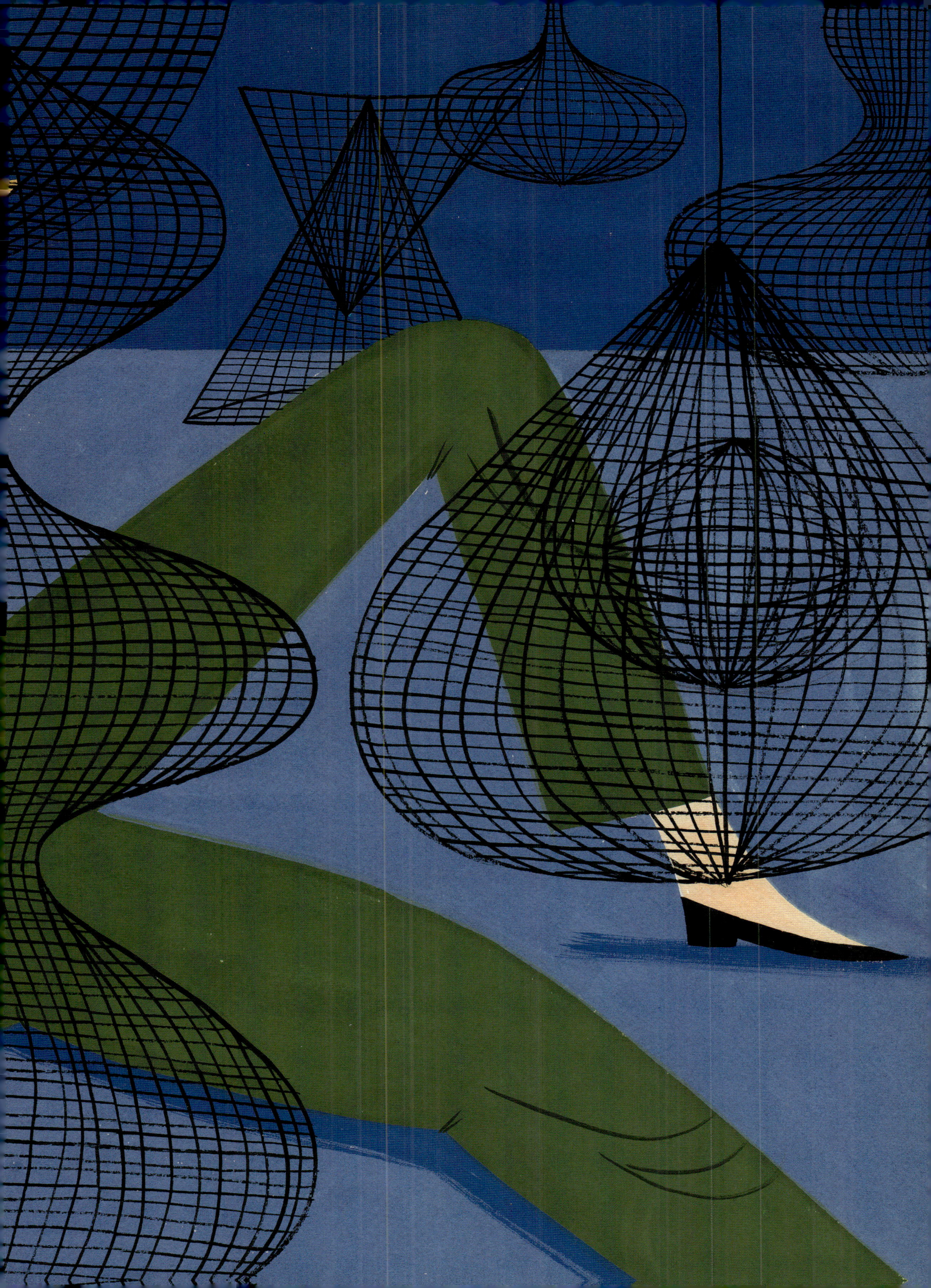

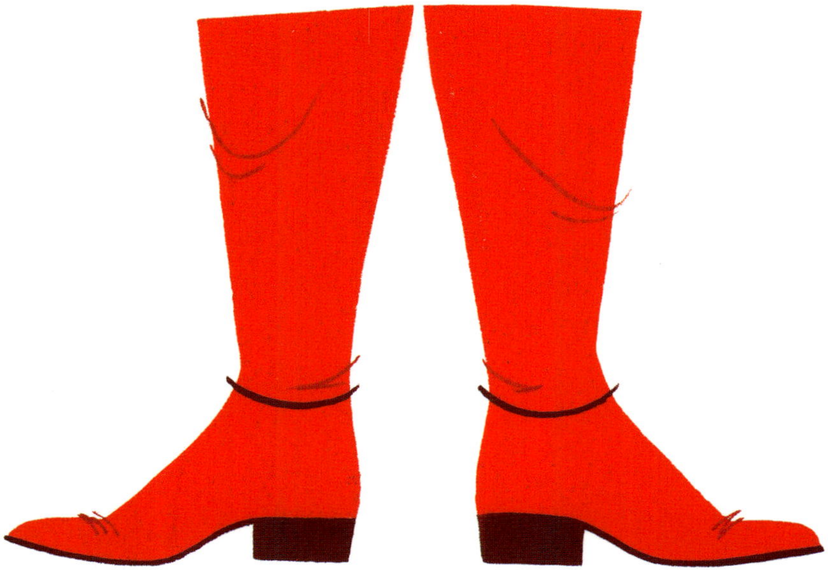

Mary Quant

and

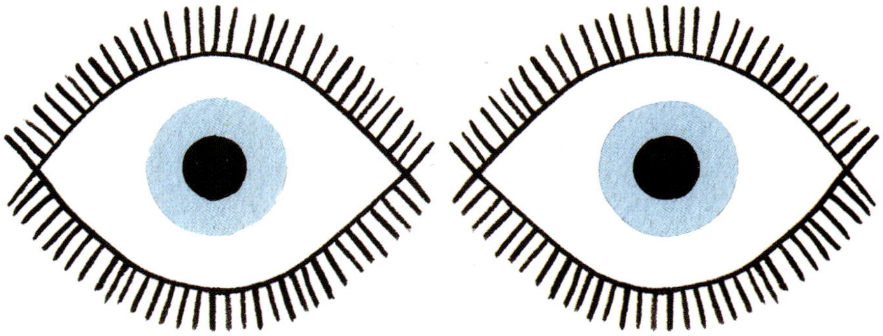

Twiggy

"The fashionable woman wears clothes. The clothes don't wear her."

"At sixteen, I was a funny, skinny little thing, all eyelashes and legs. And then, suddenly people told me it was gorgeous. I thought they had gone mad."

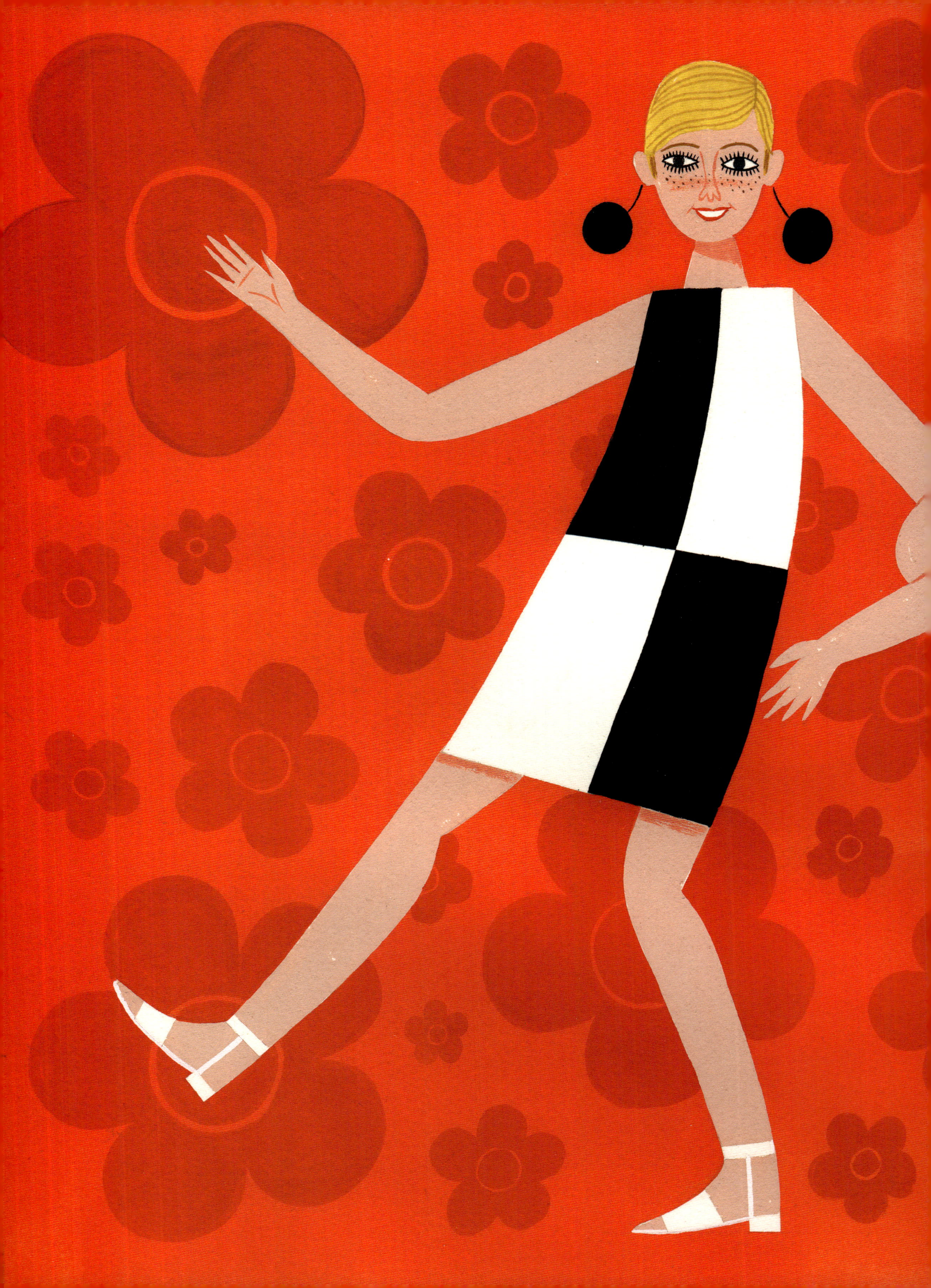

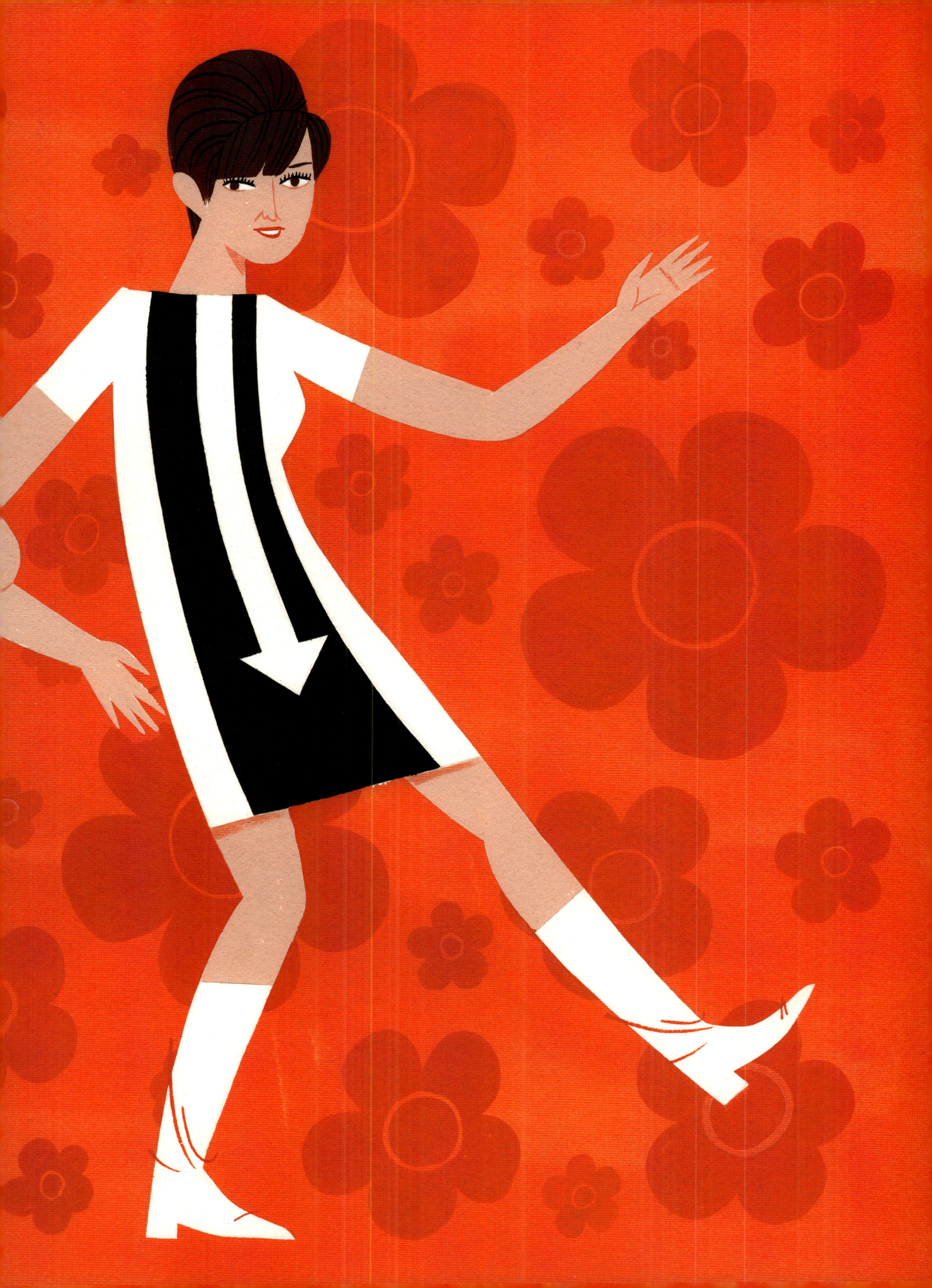

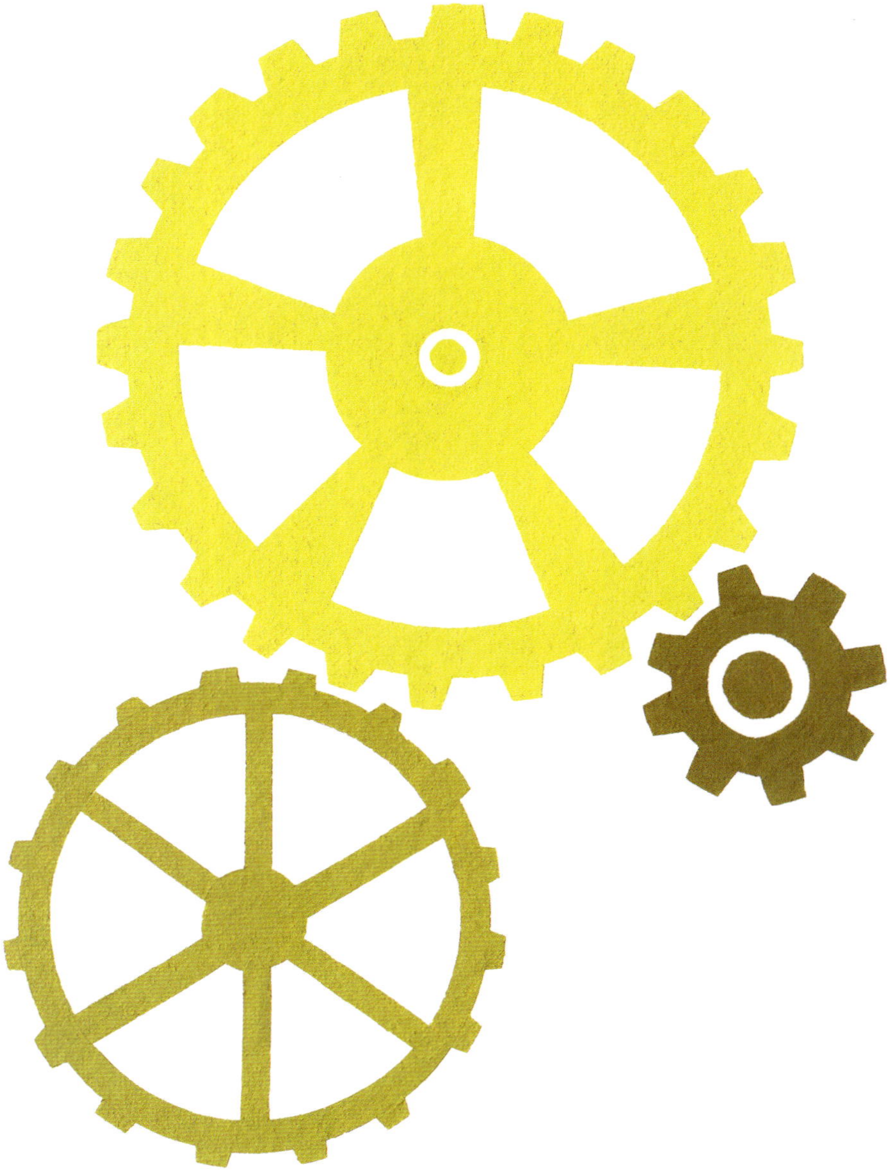

Louise Nevelson

"I never feel age. ... If you have creative work, you don't have age or time."

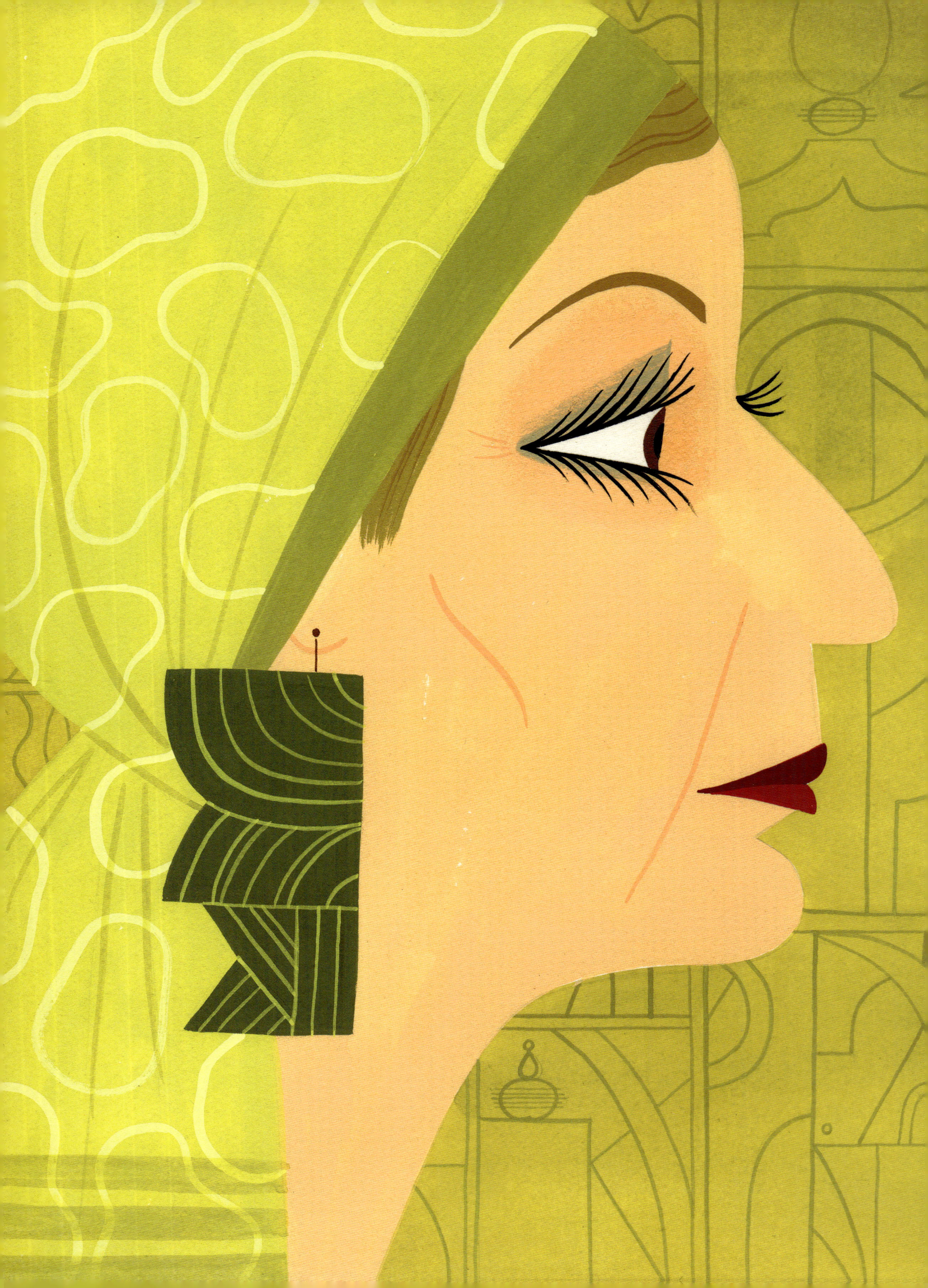

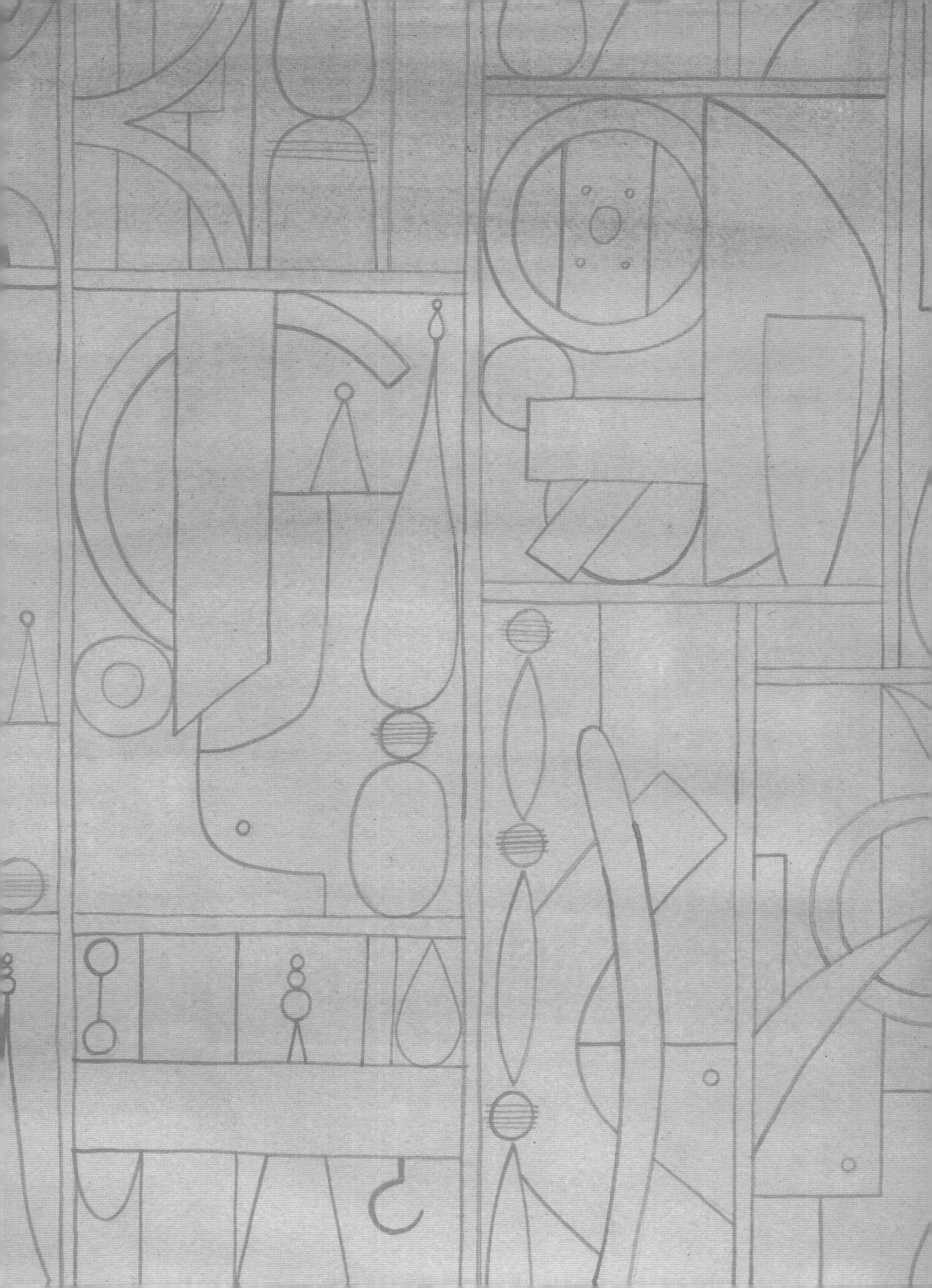

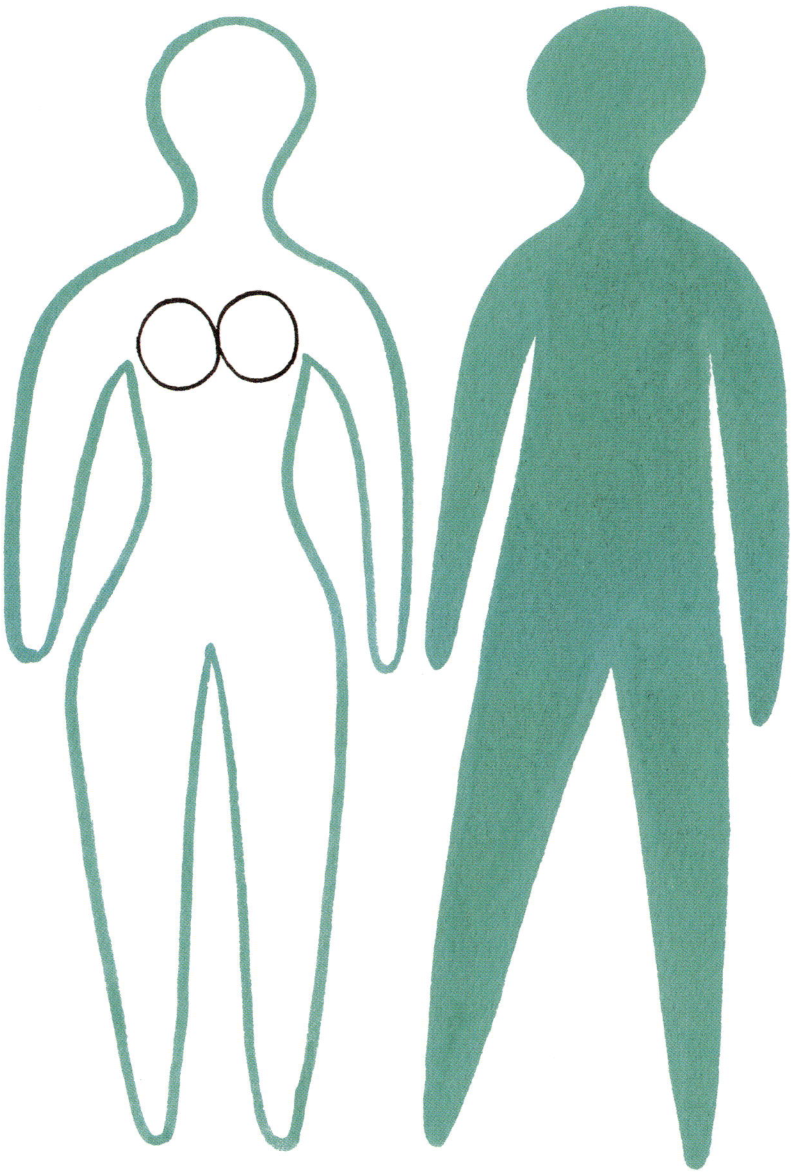

Elaine Lustig Cohen

“My gender may have been an issue for other designers, but not for my clients.”

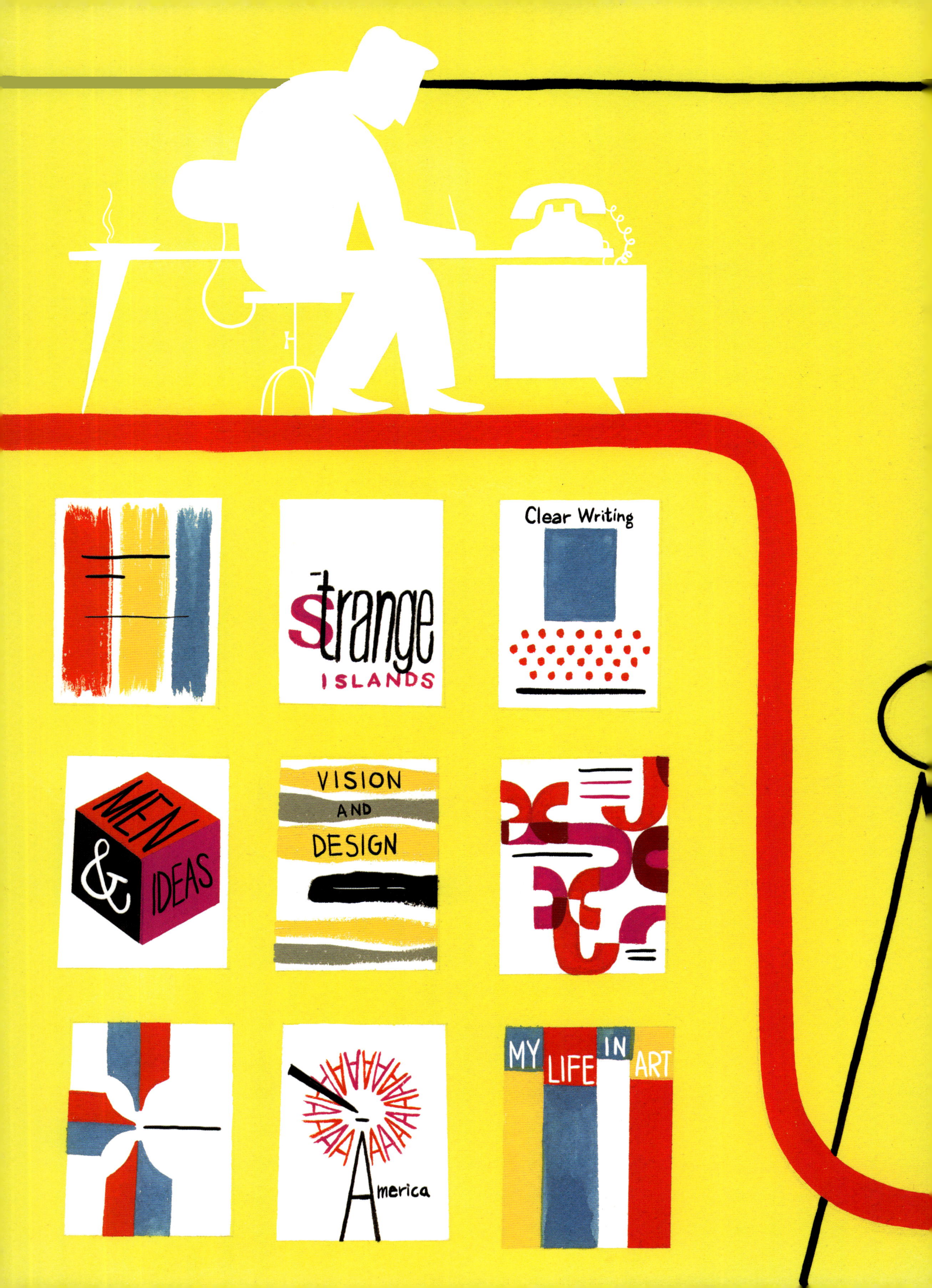

Clear Writing
strange
ISLANDS
MEN
&
IDEAS
VISION
AND
DESIGN
MY
LIFE
IN
ART
America

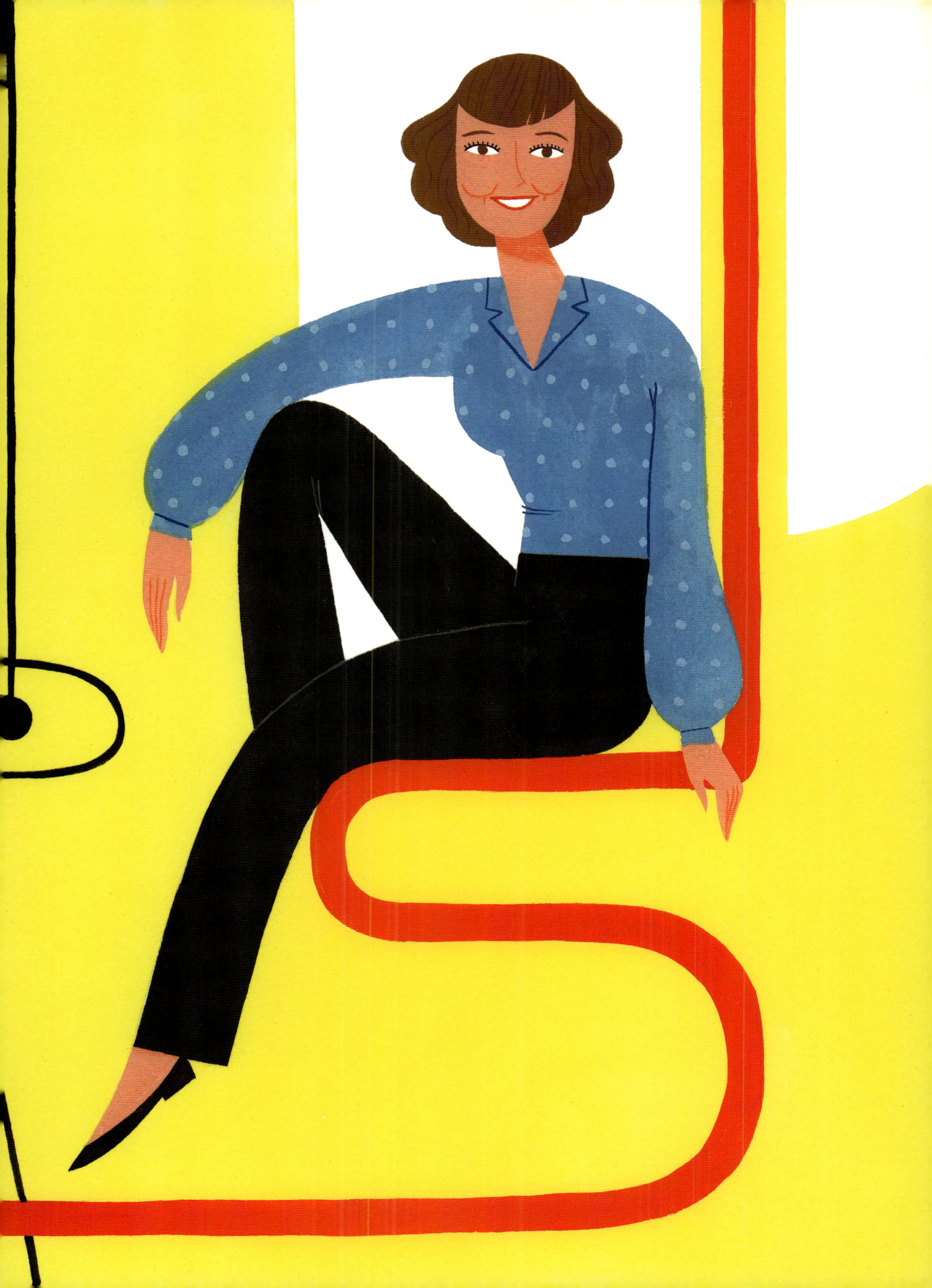

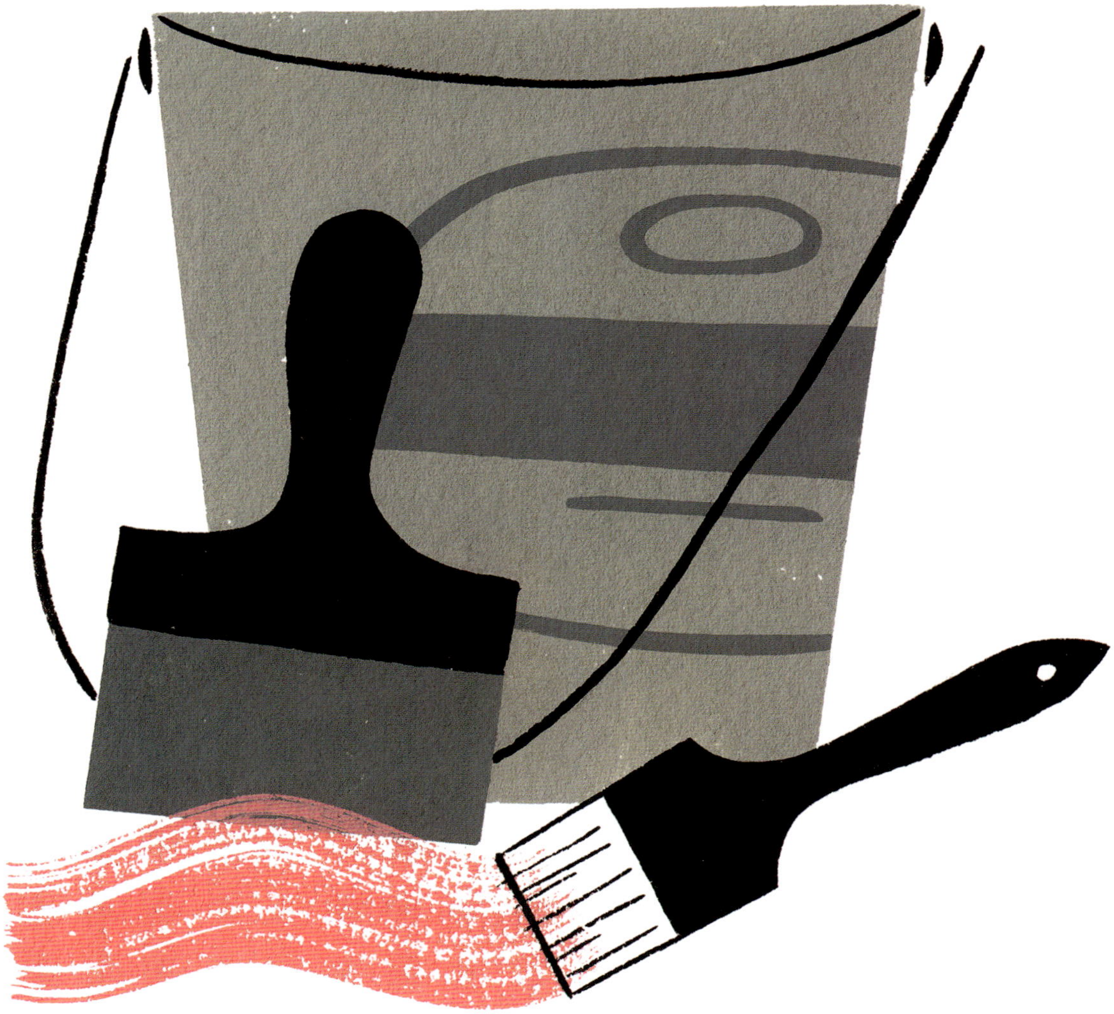

Helen Frankenthaler

“Go against the rules or ignore the rules. That is what invention is about.”

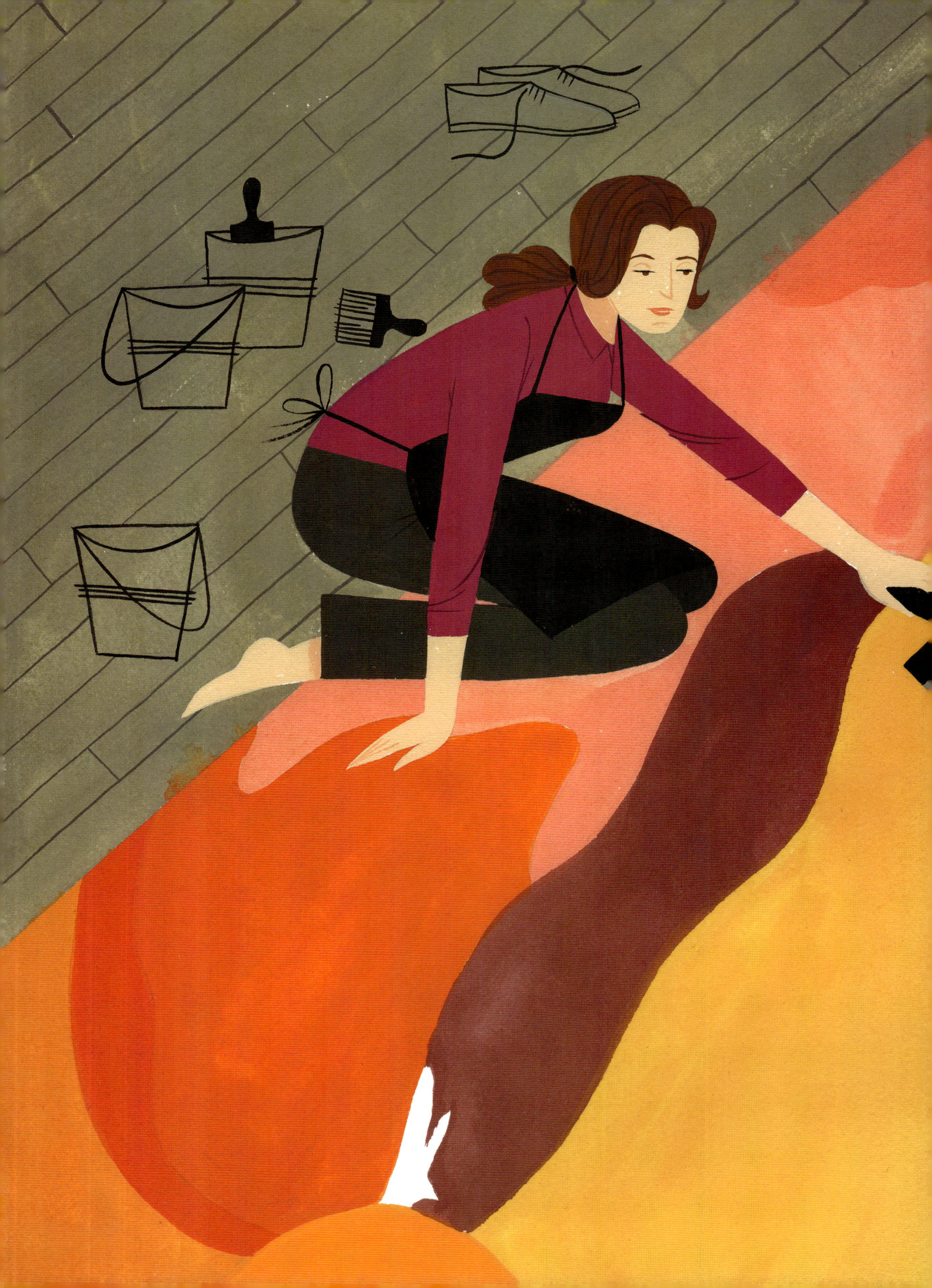

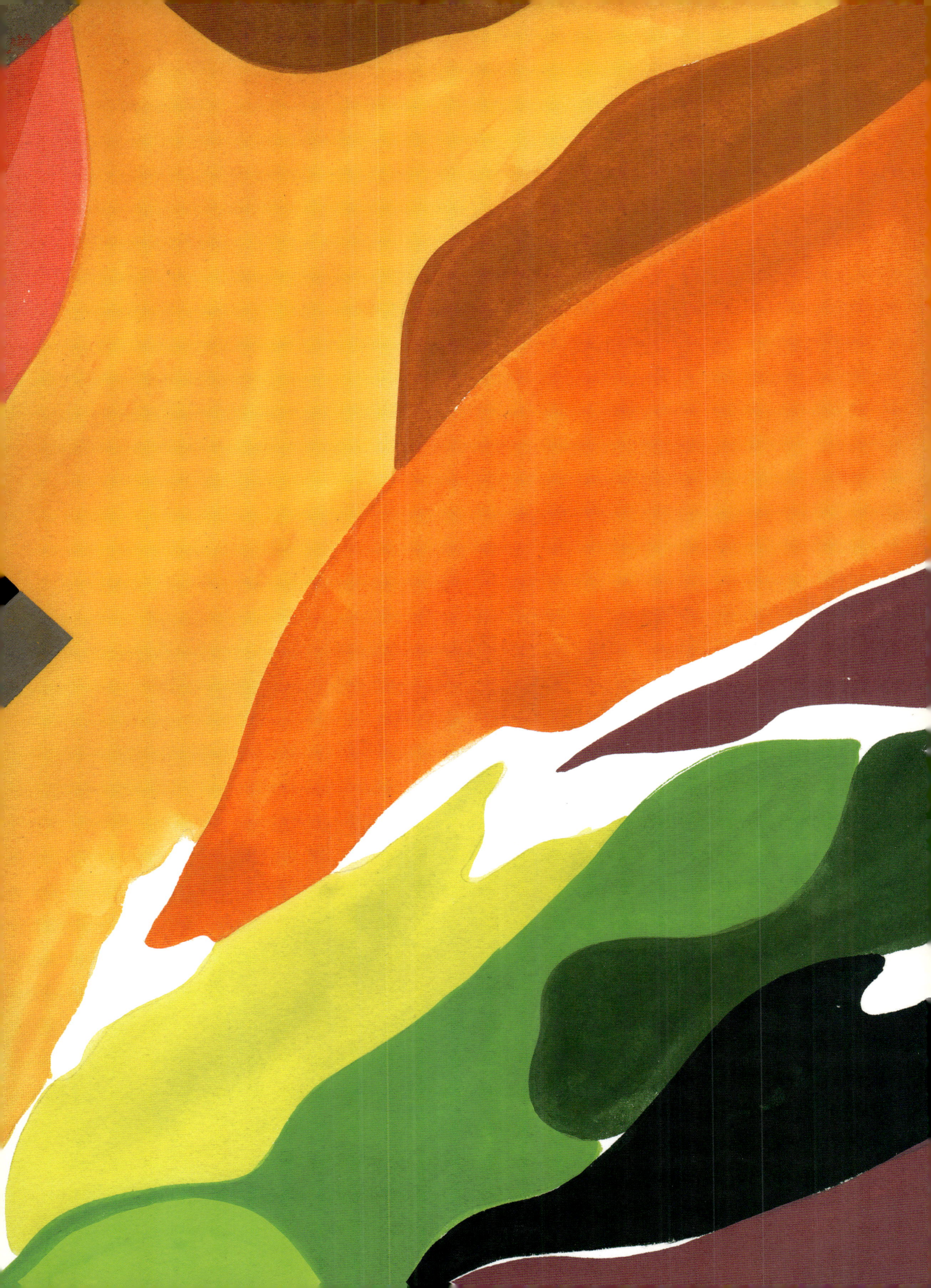

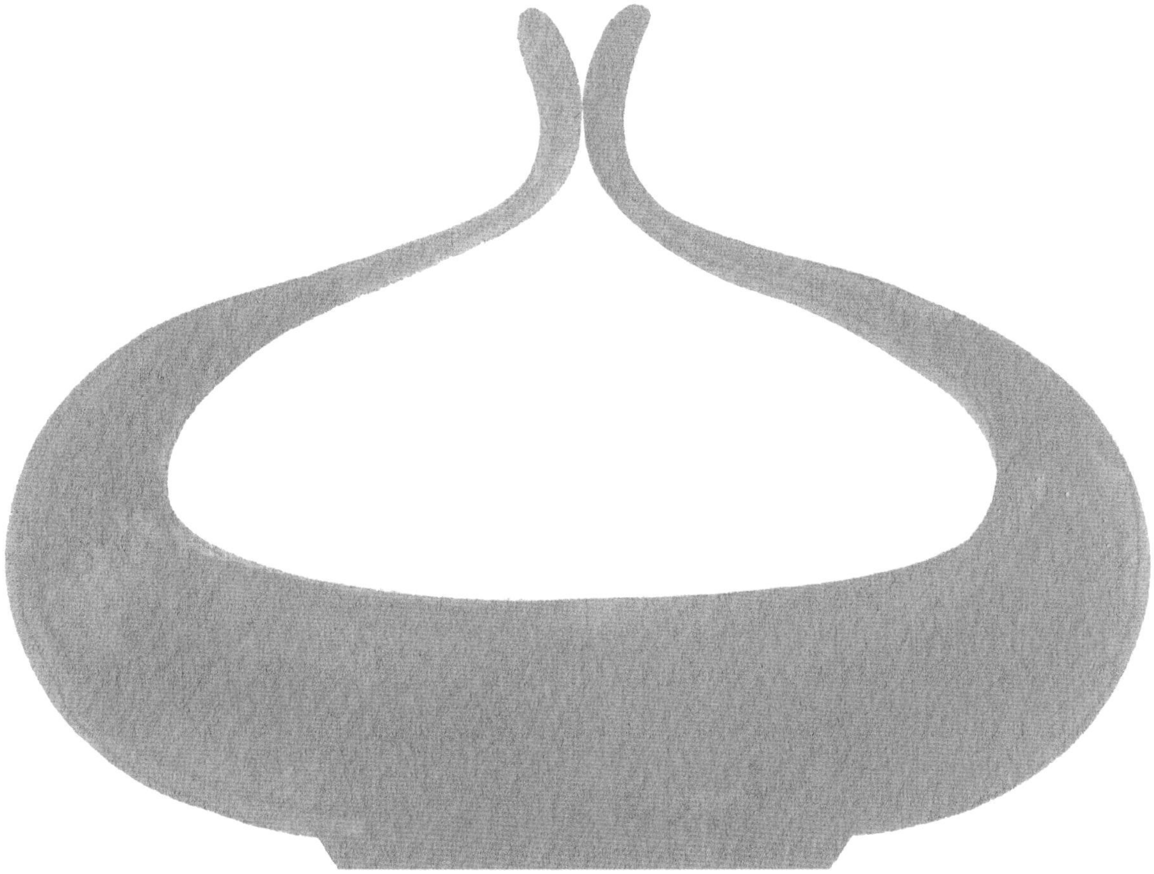

Eva Zeisel

“Beautiful things make people happy.”

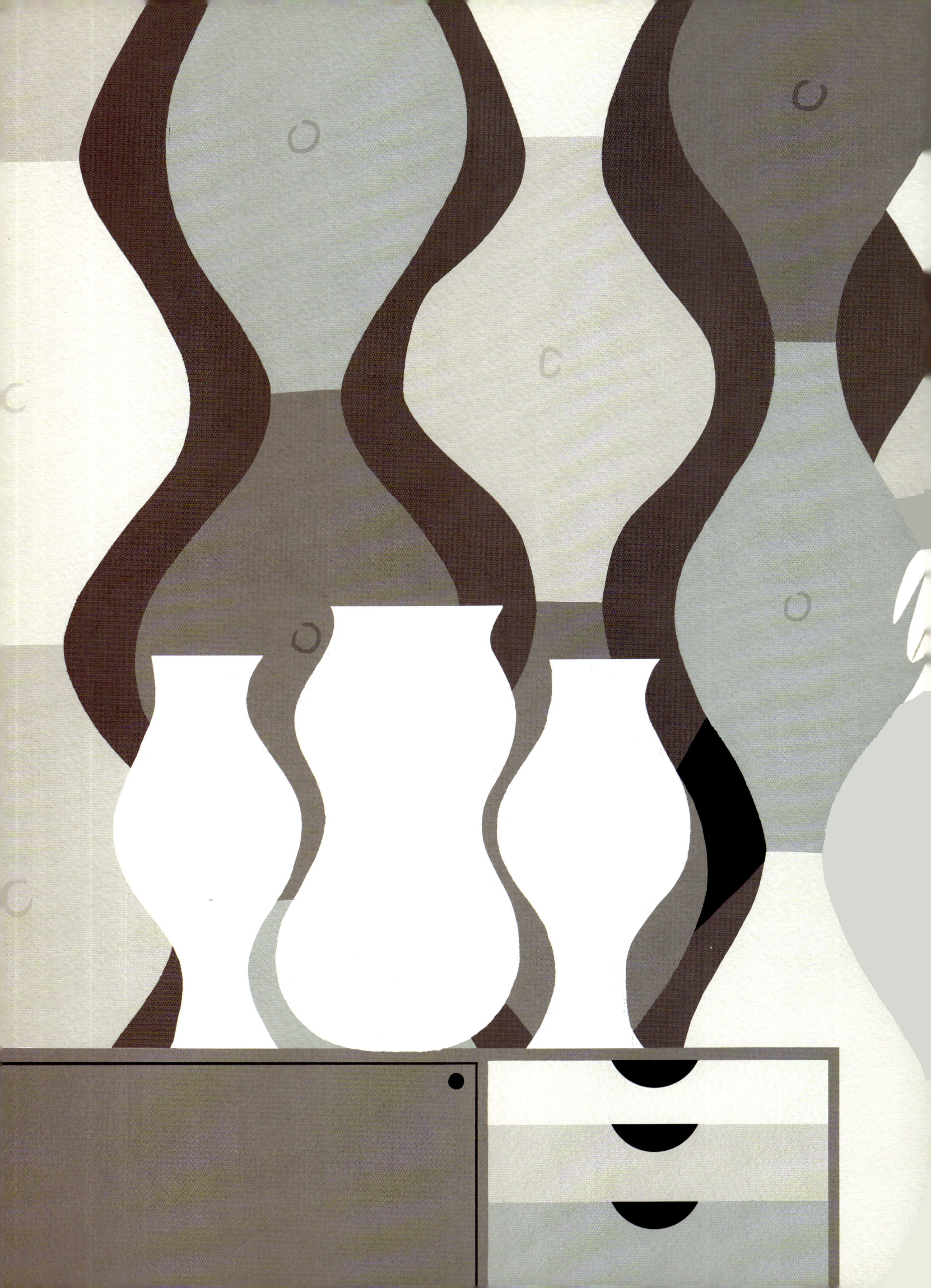

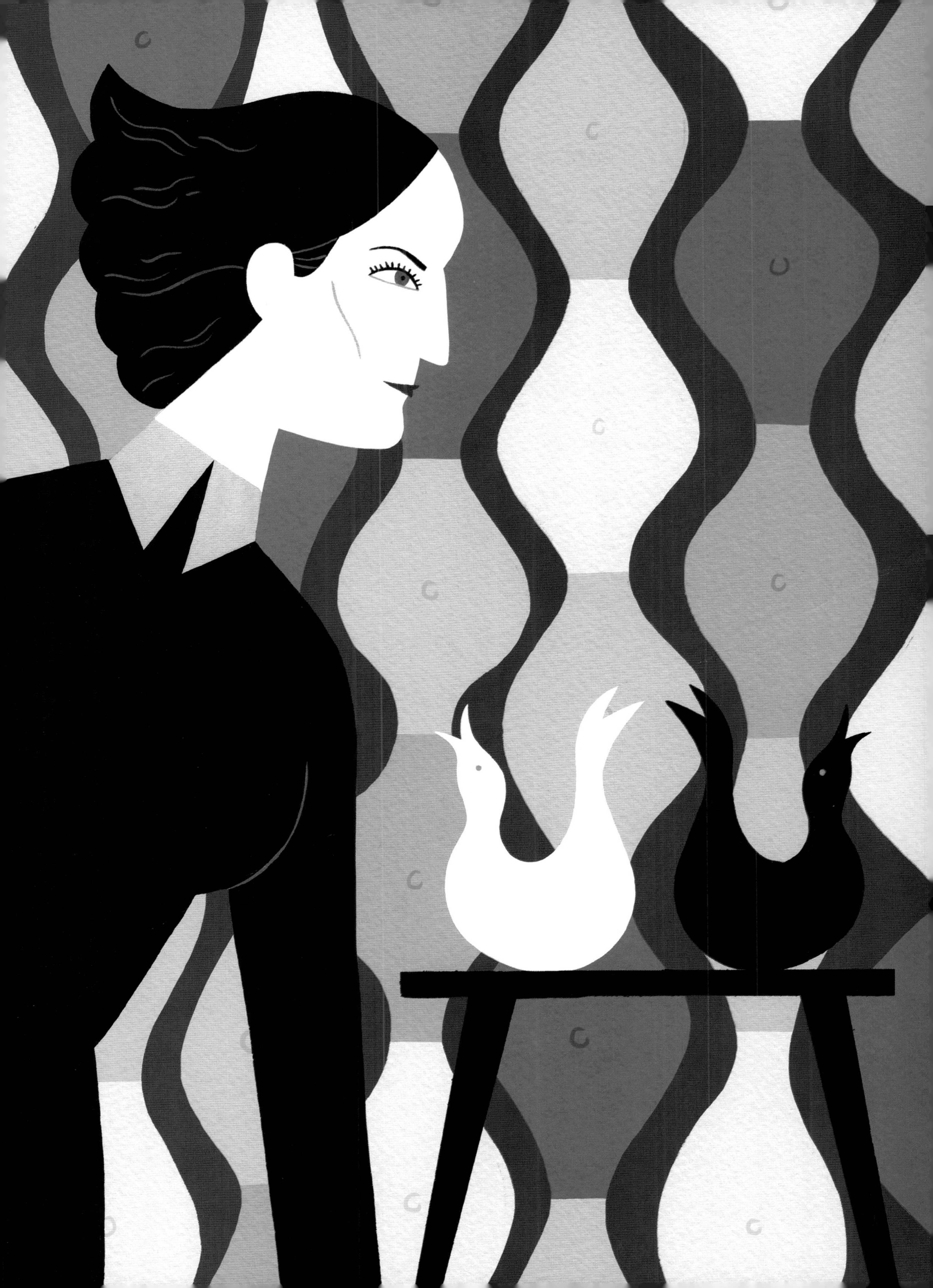

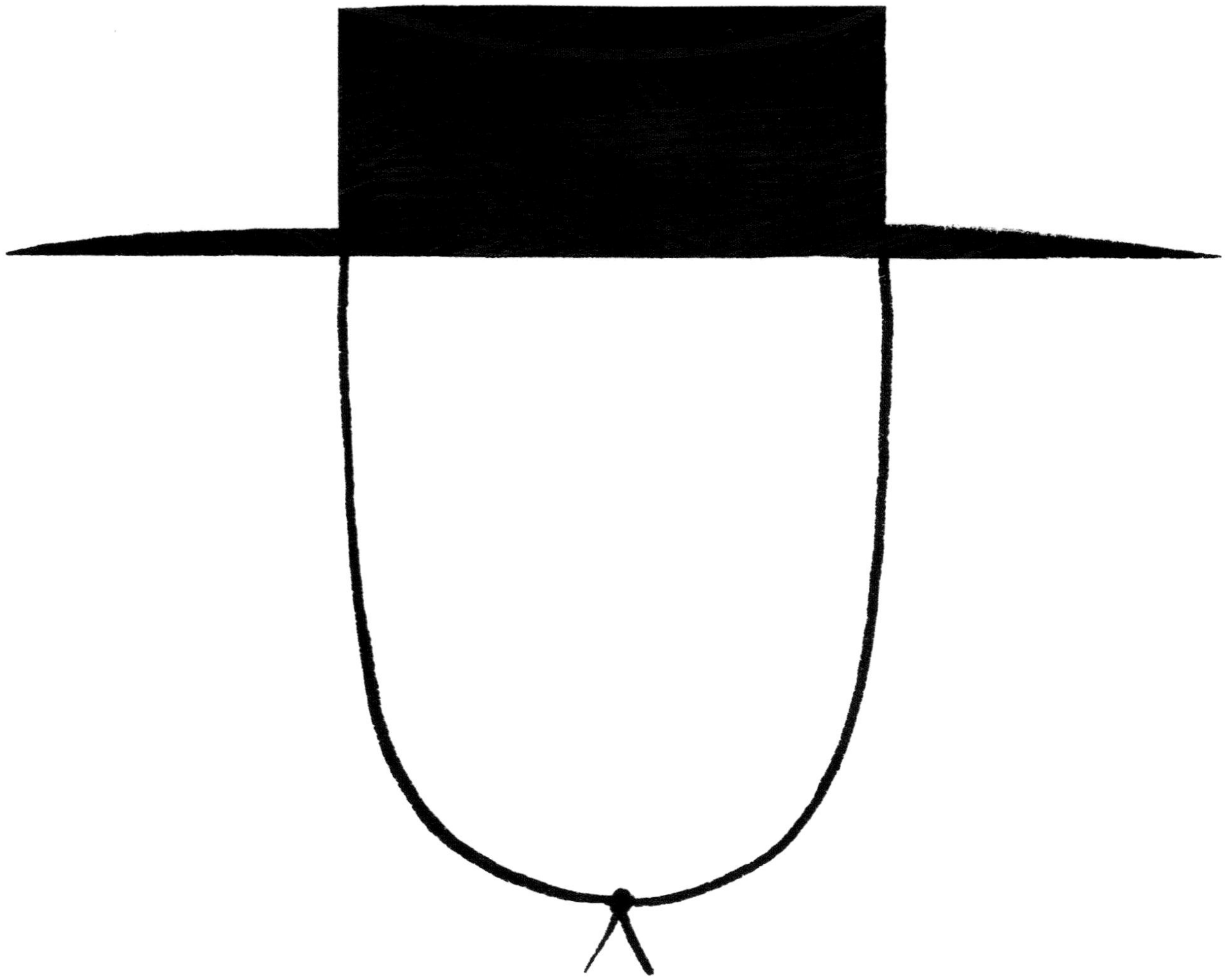

Georgia O'Keeffe

"I found I could say things with color and shapes that I couldn't say any other way—things I had no words for."

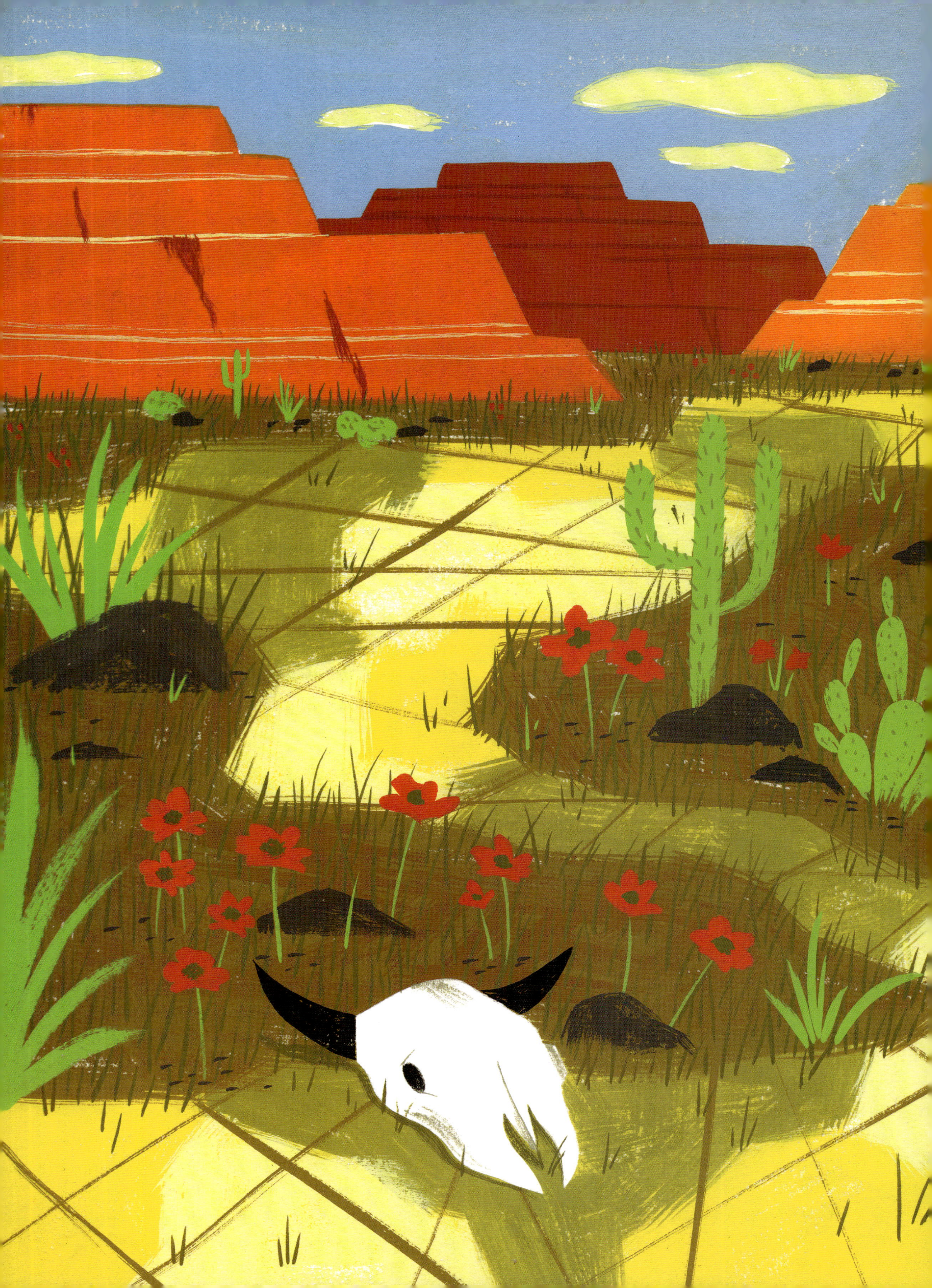

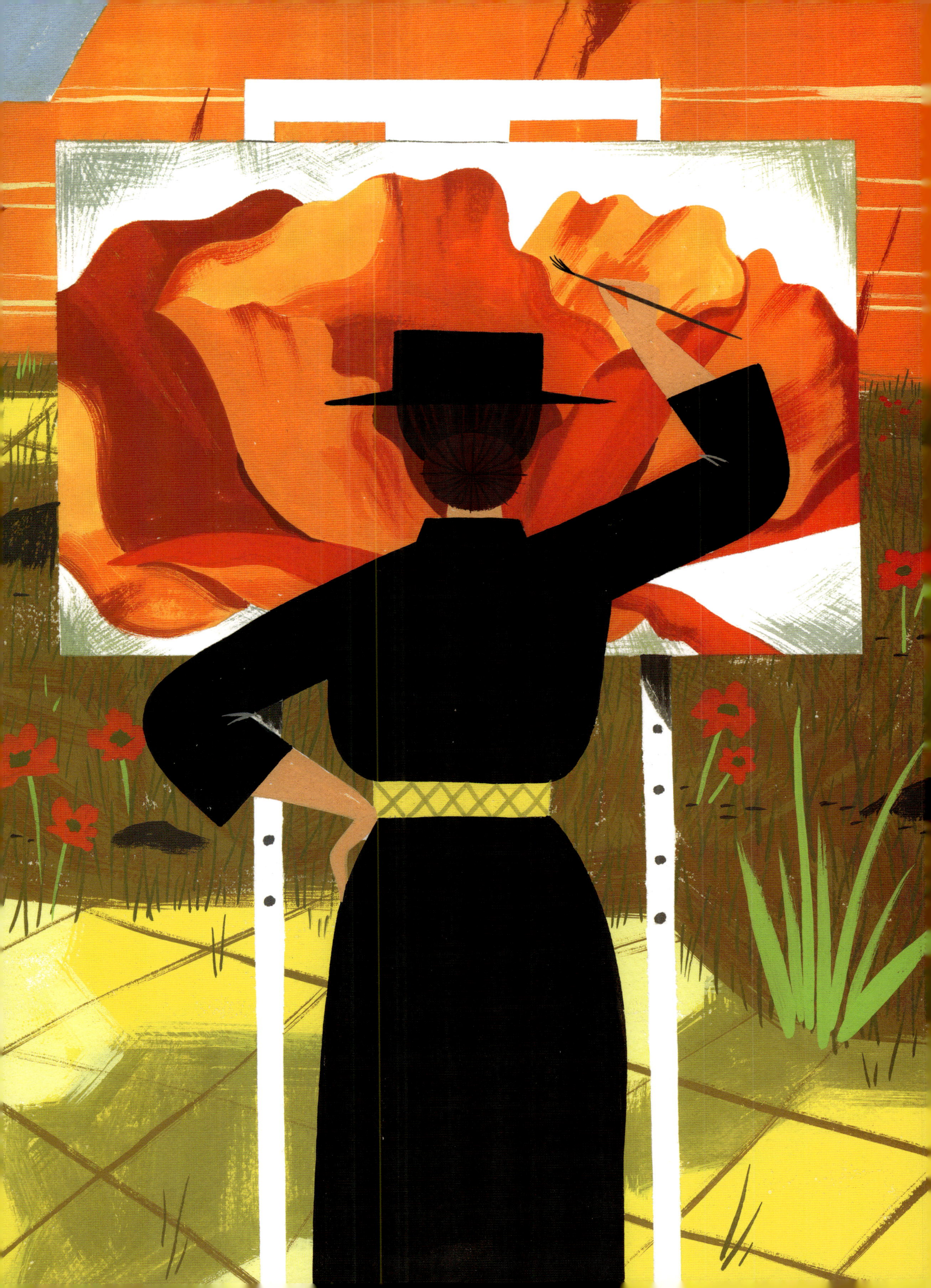

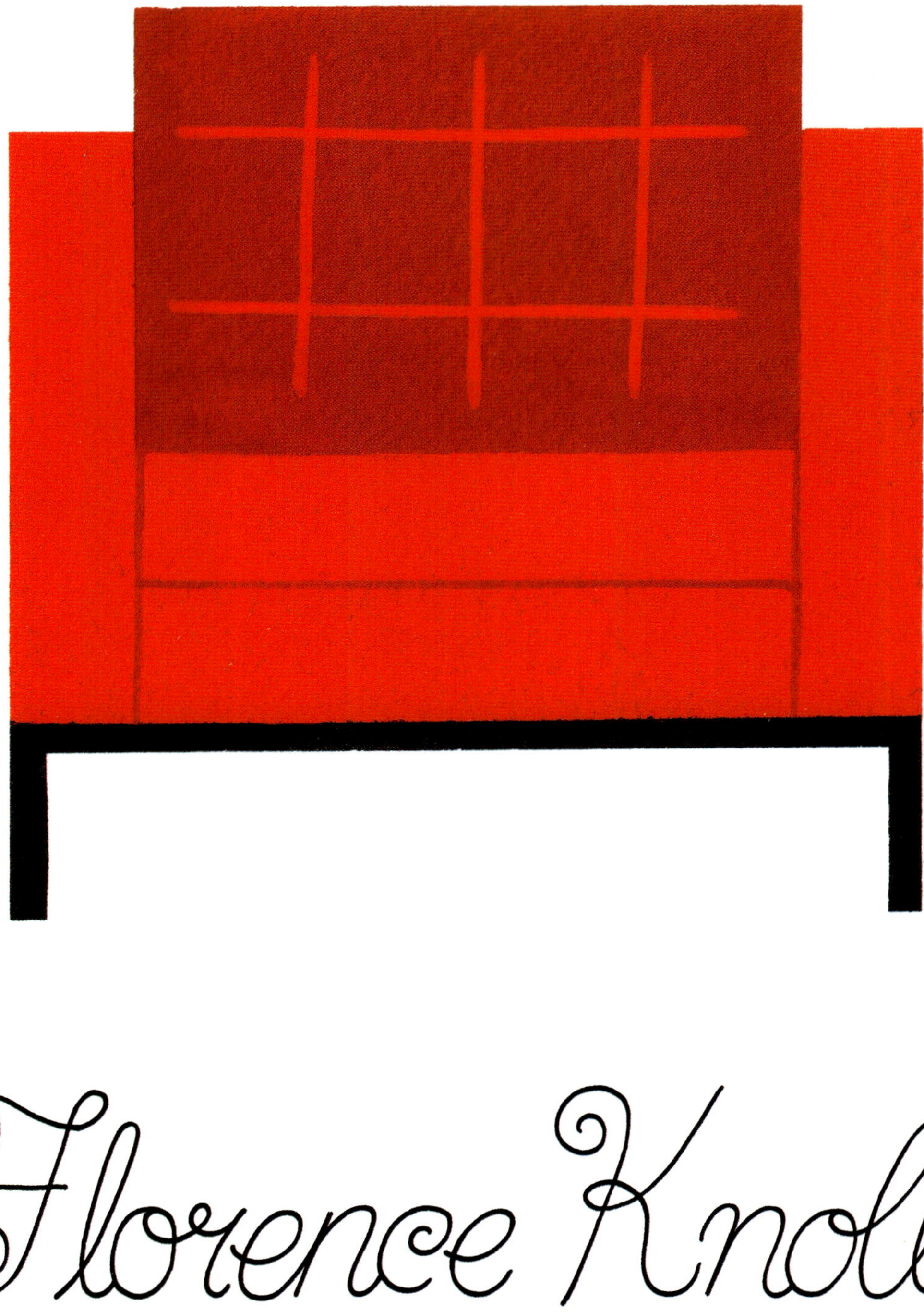

Florence Knoll

“Good design is good business.”

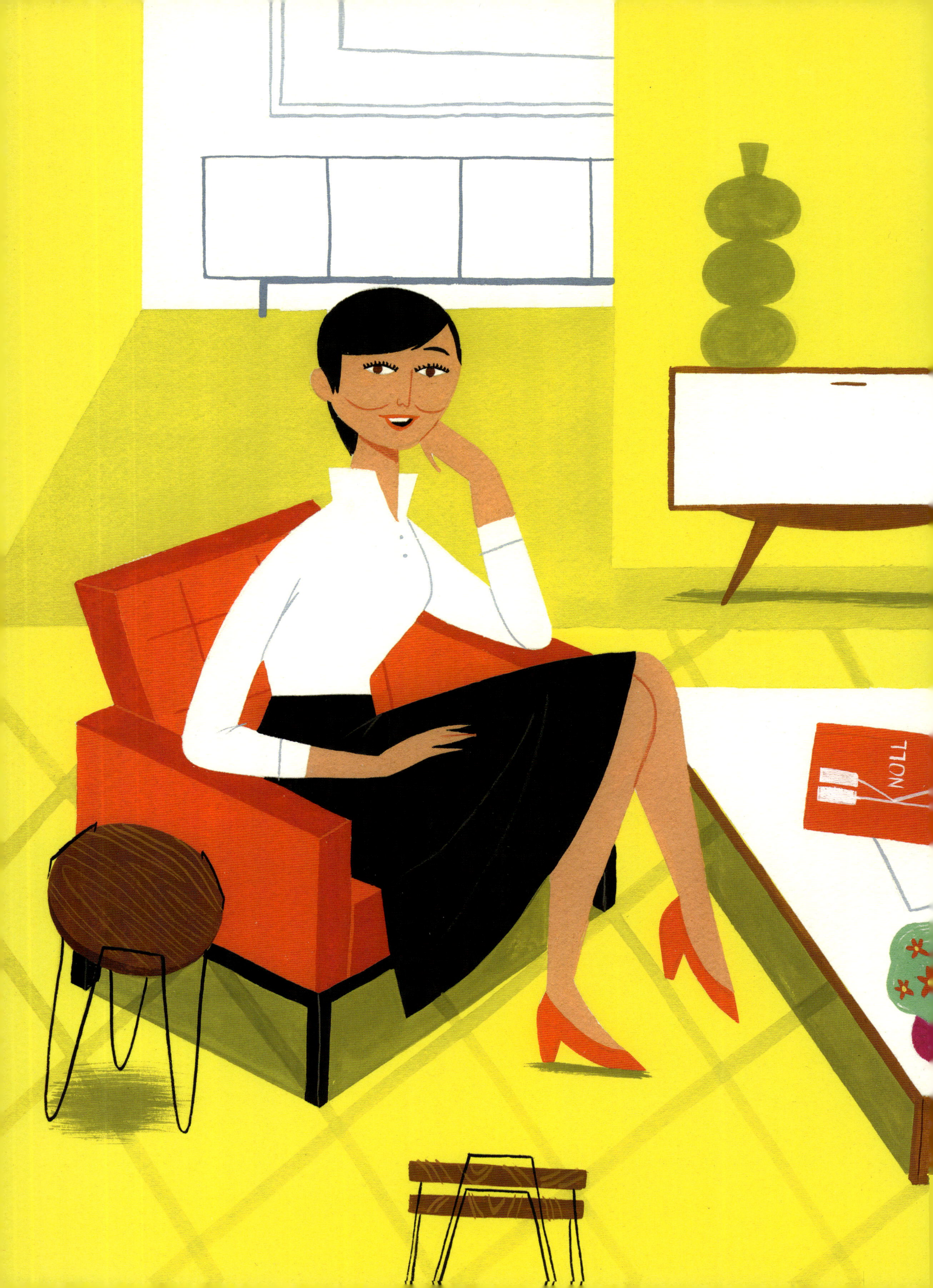
NOLL

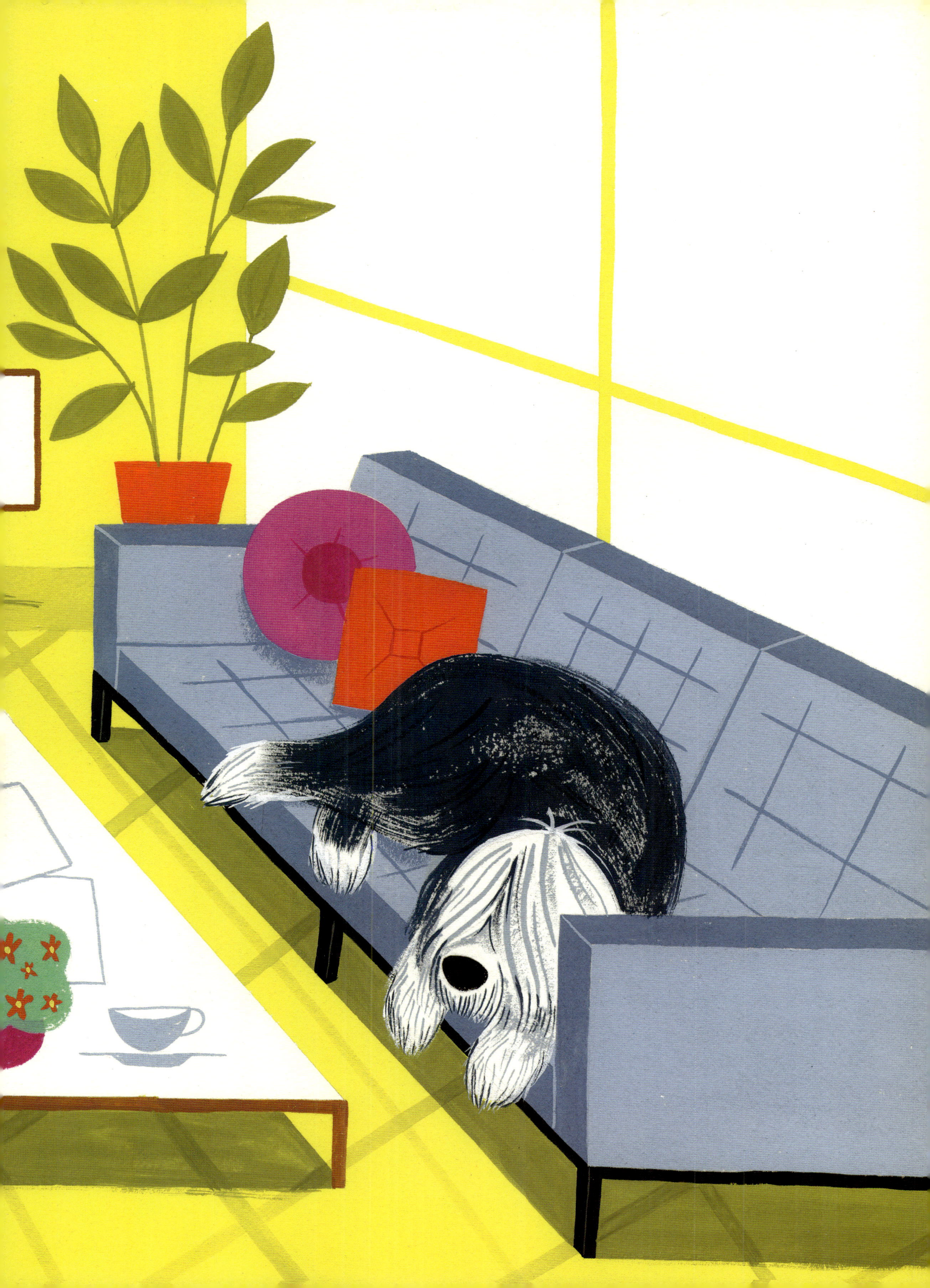

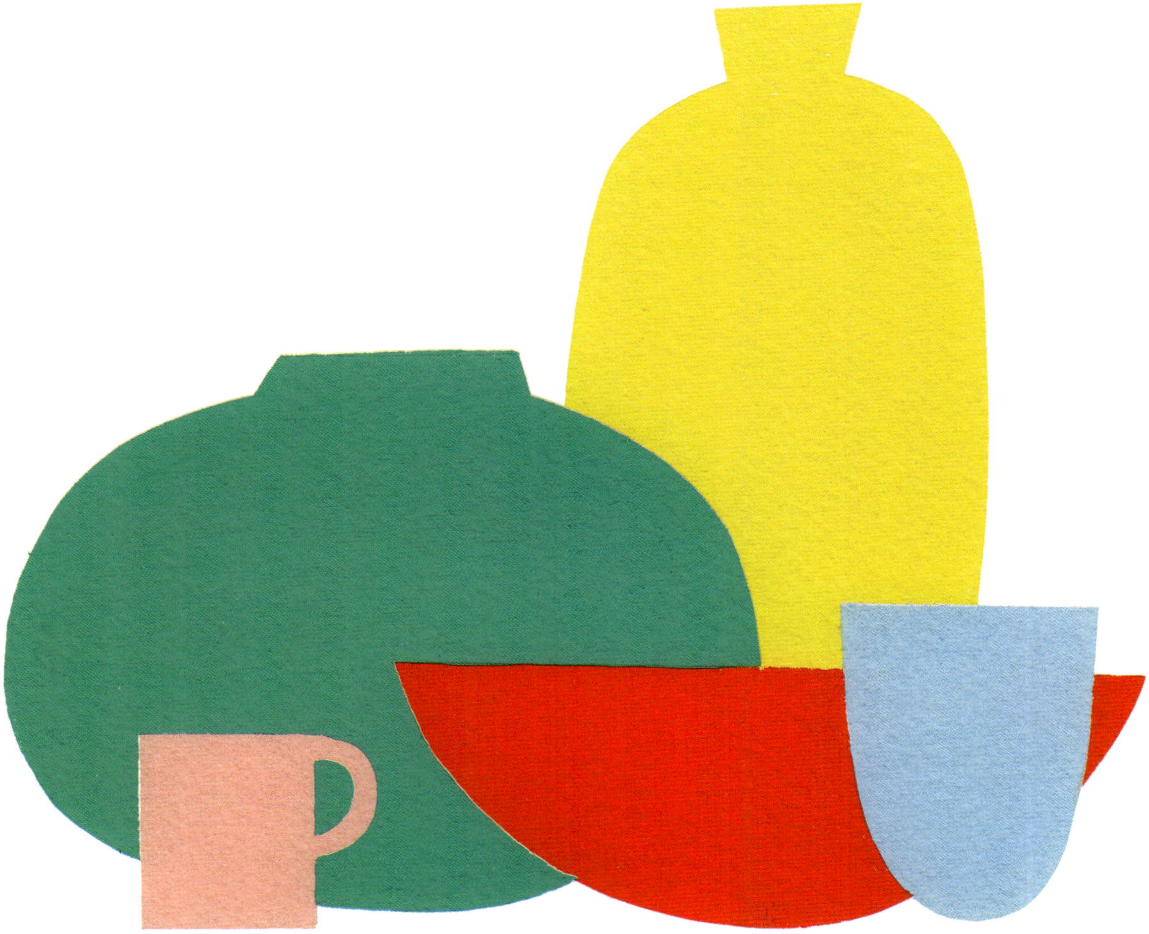

Edith Heath

"I was trying to do something that was more egalitarian rather than aristocratic."

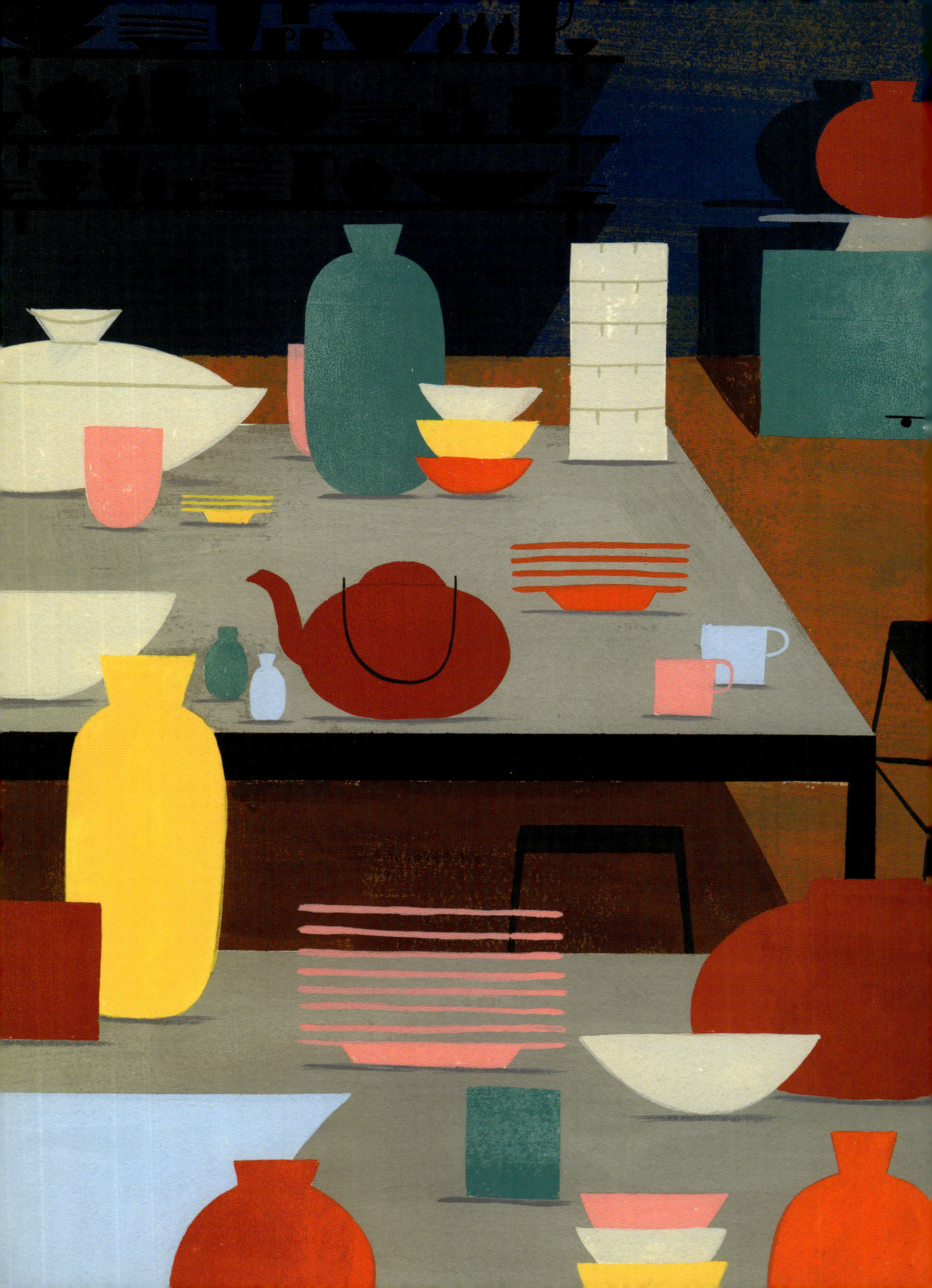

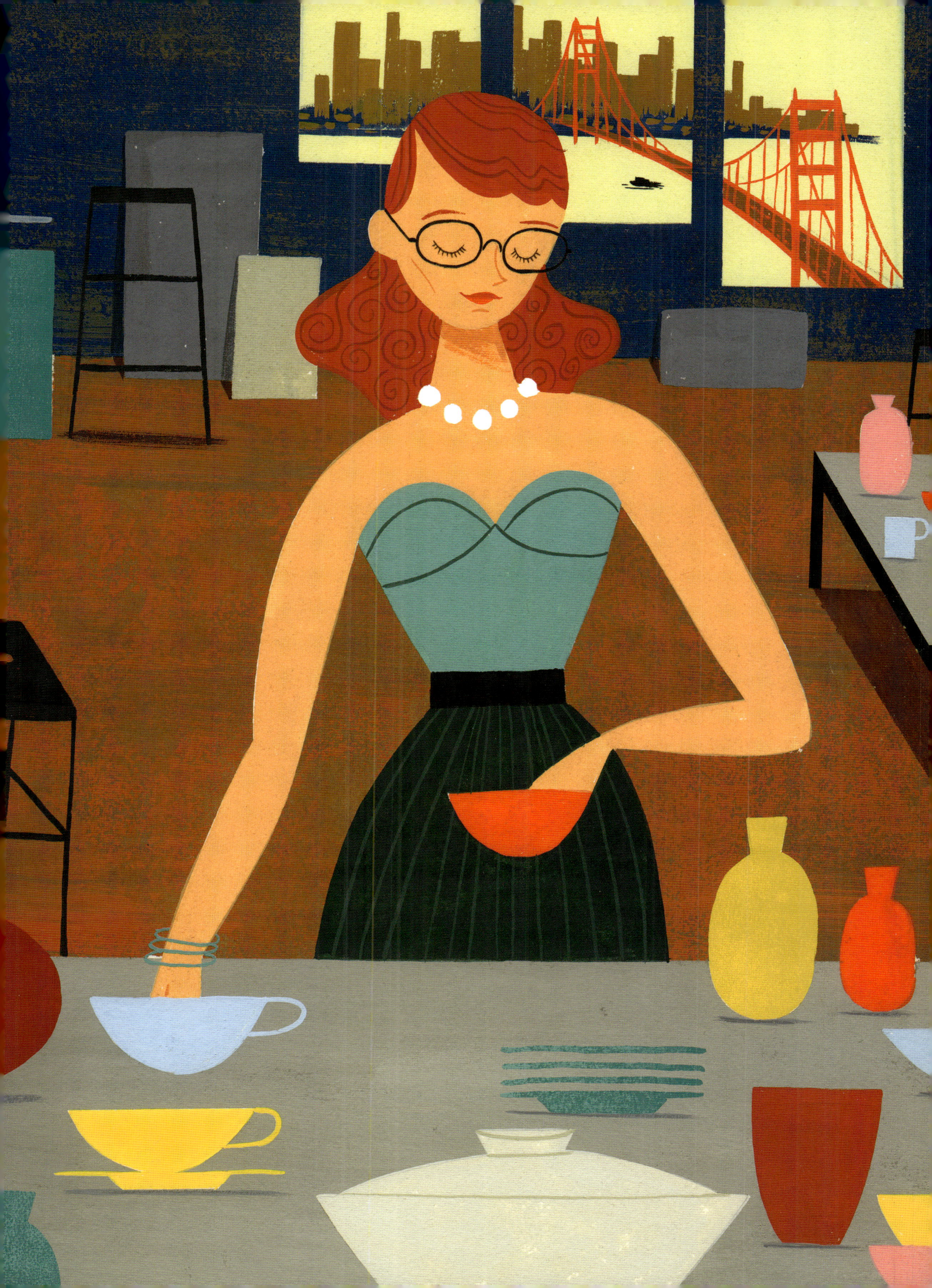

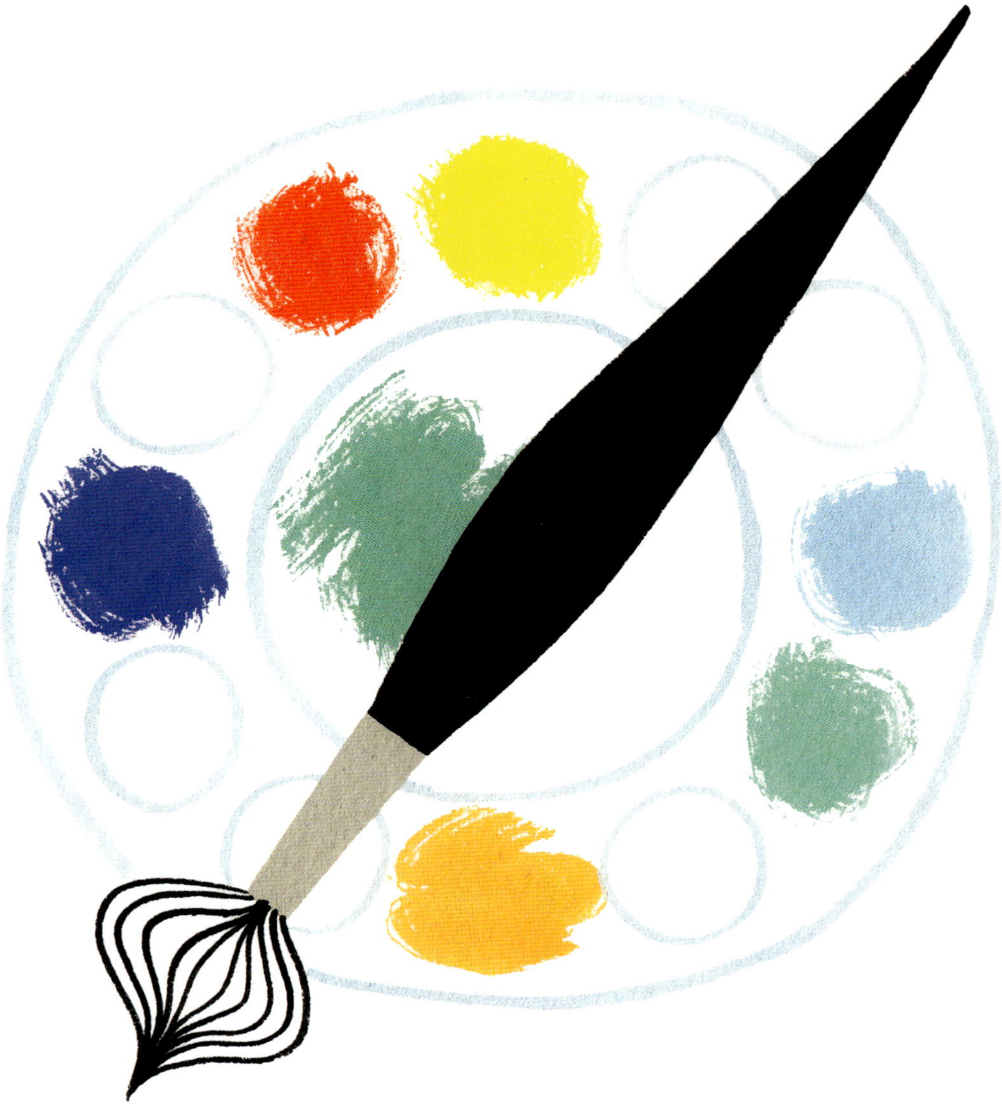

Alma Thomas

"What I would rather do is to paint something beautiful."

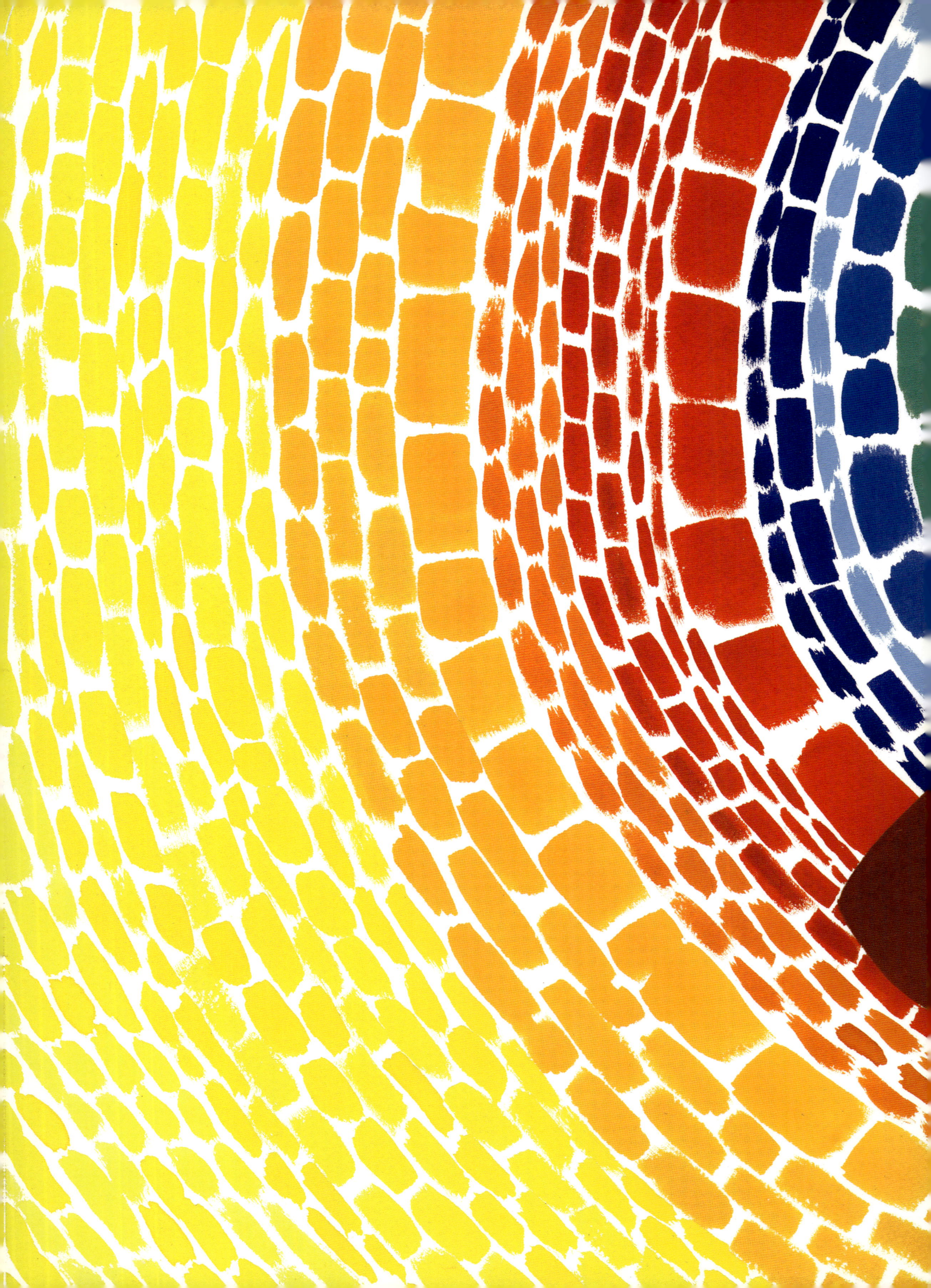

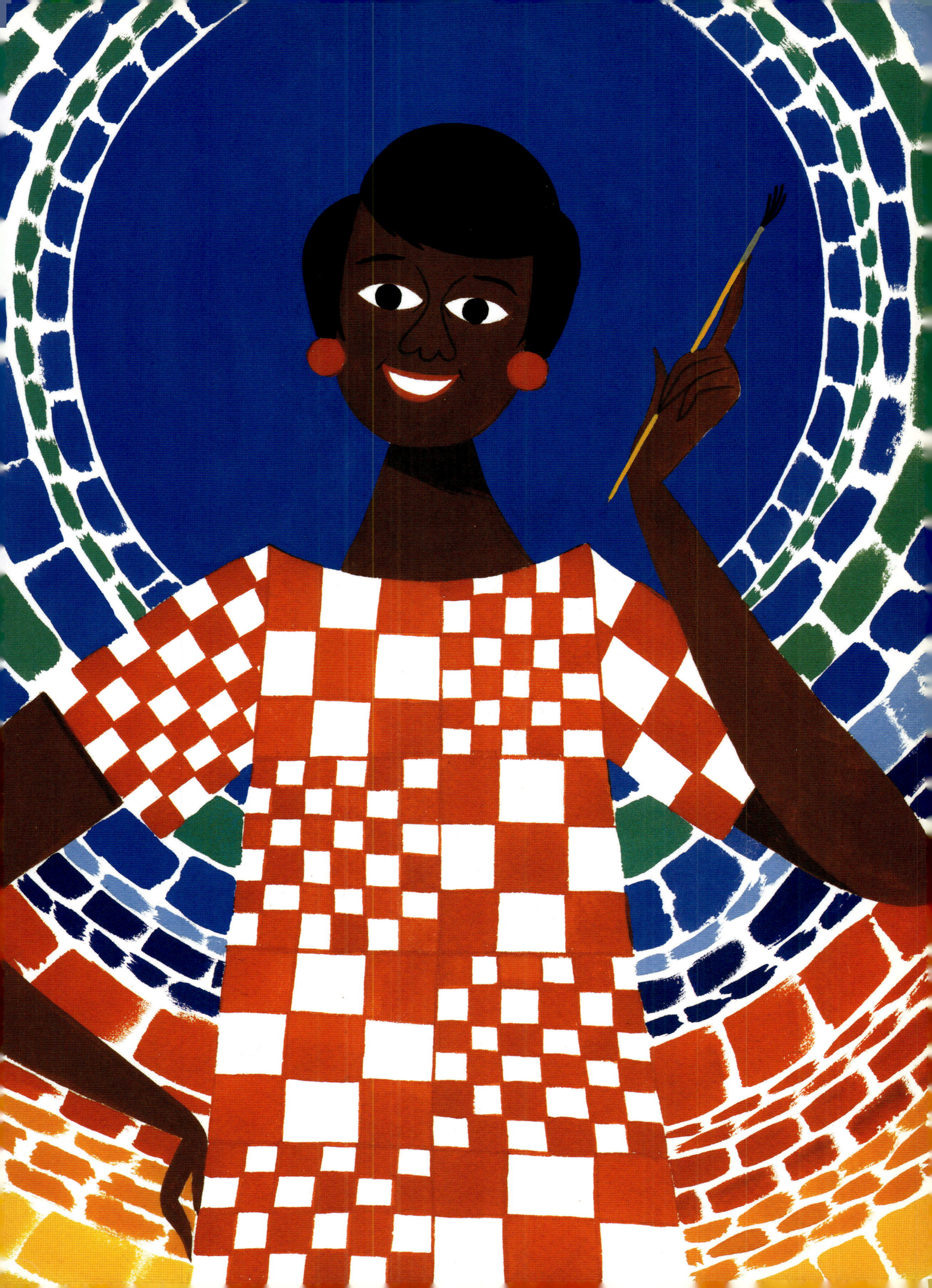

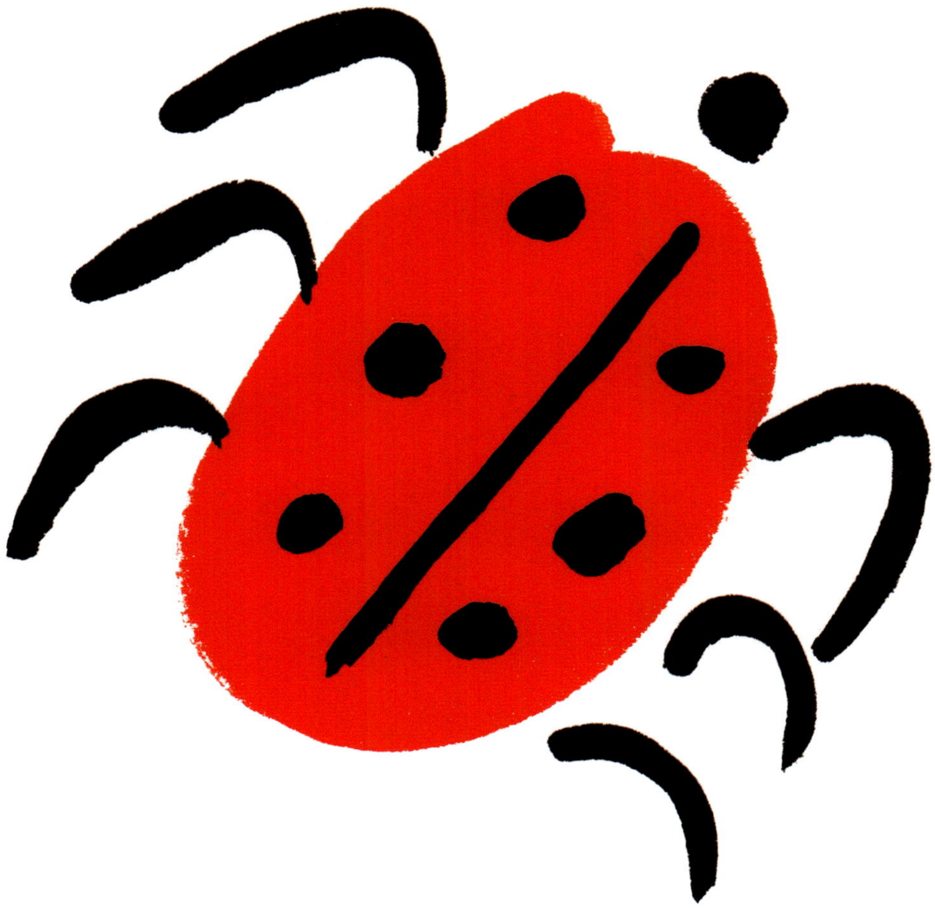

Vera Neumann

"As a child
drawing
wildflowers, ferns,
and butterflies ...
I dreamed that
someday I would
be an artist."

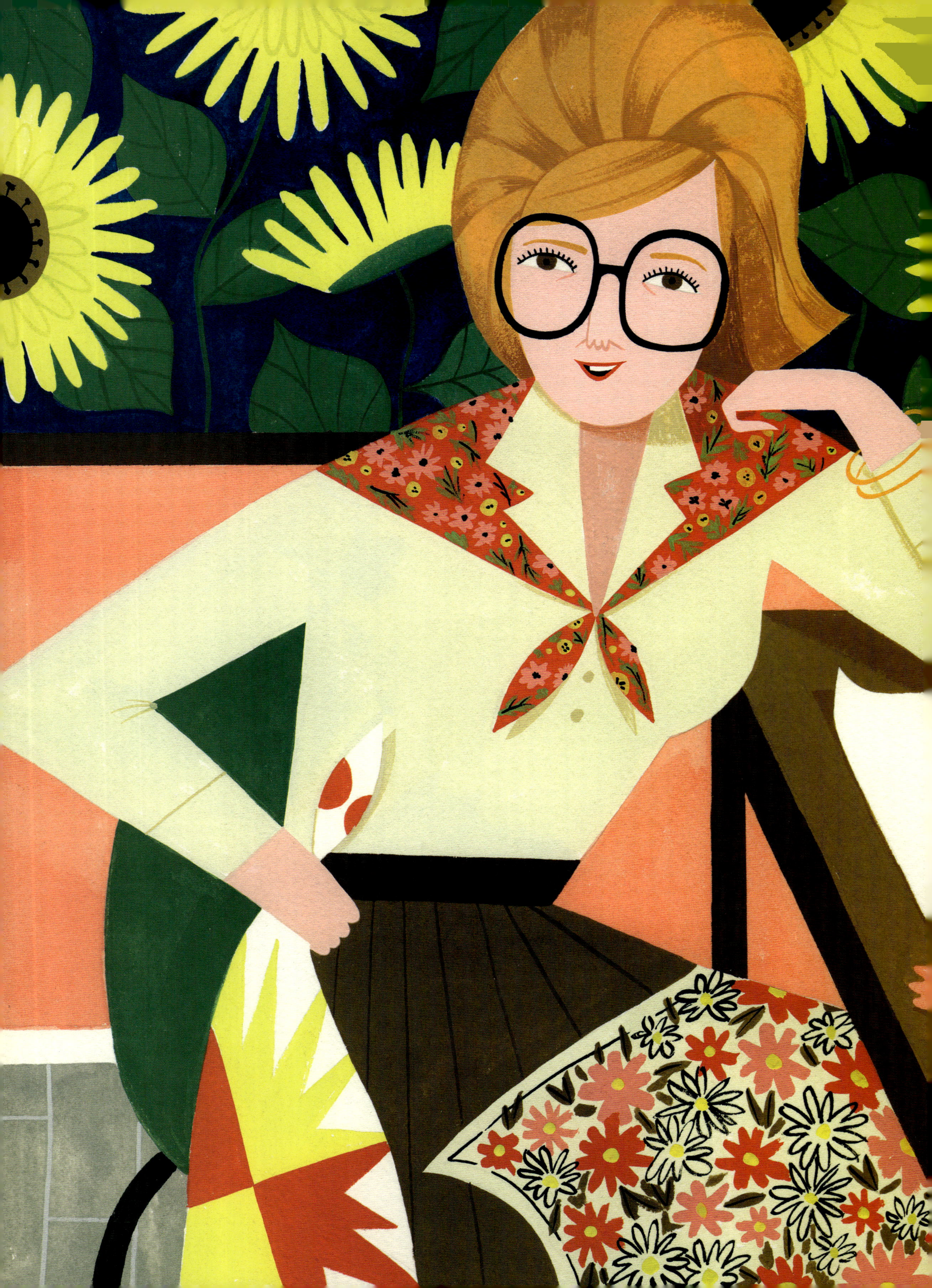

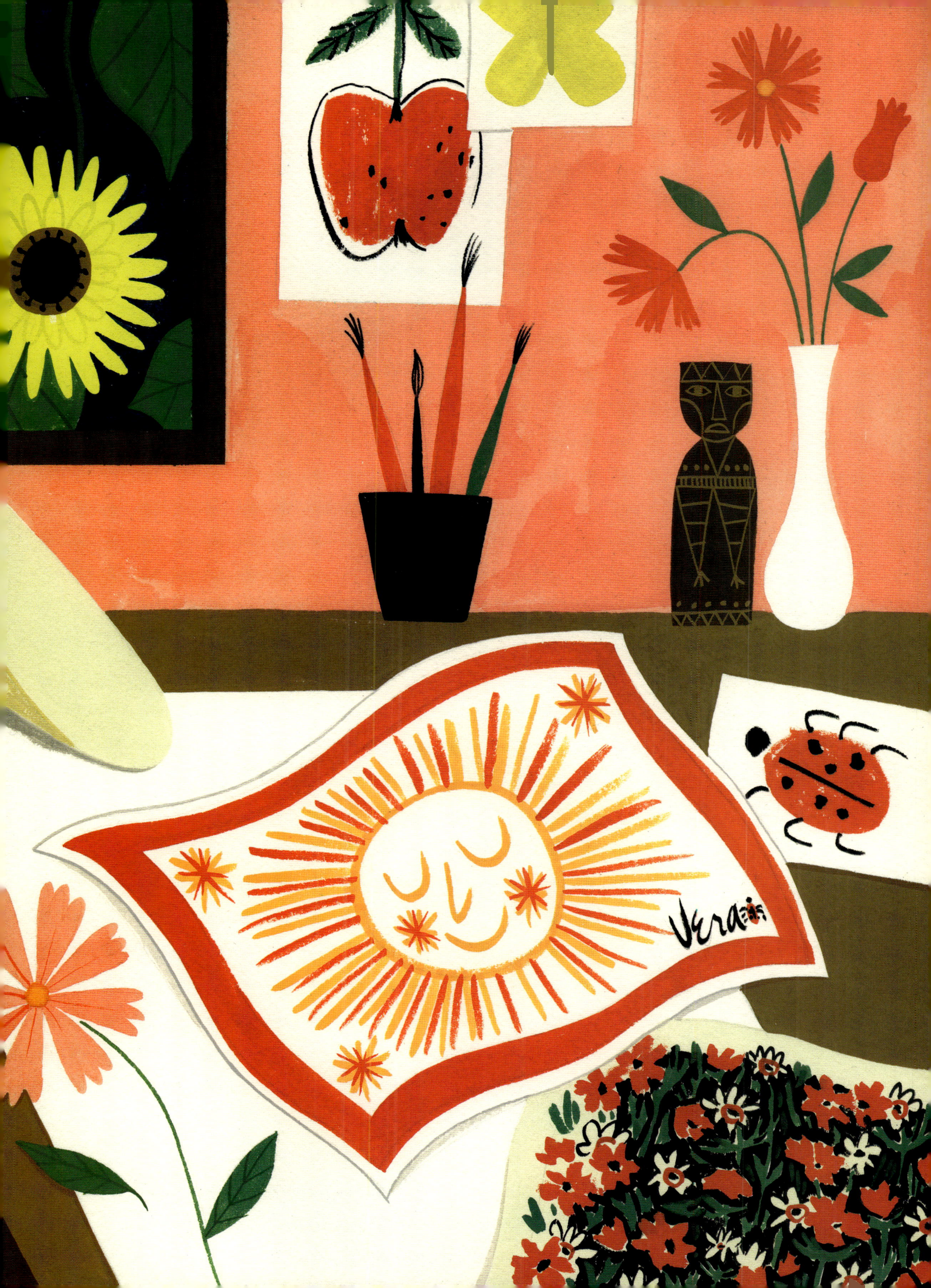
Vera

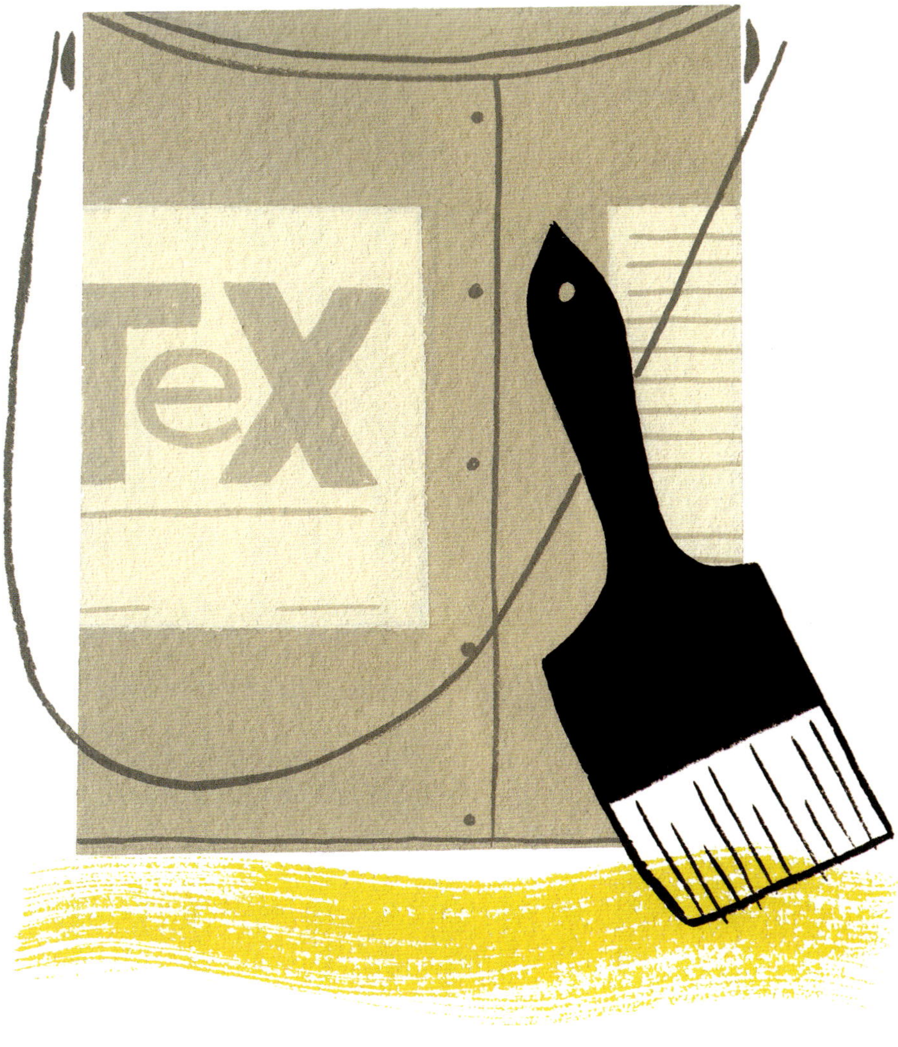

Eva Hesse

“In my inner soul art and life are inseparable.”

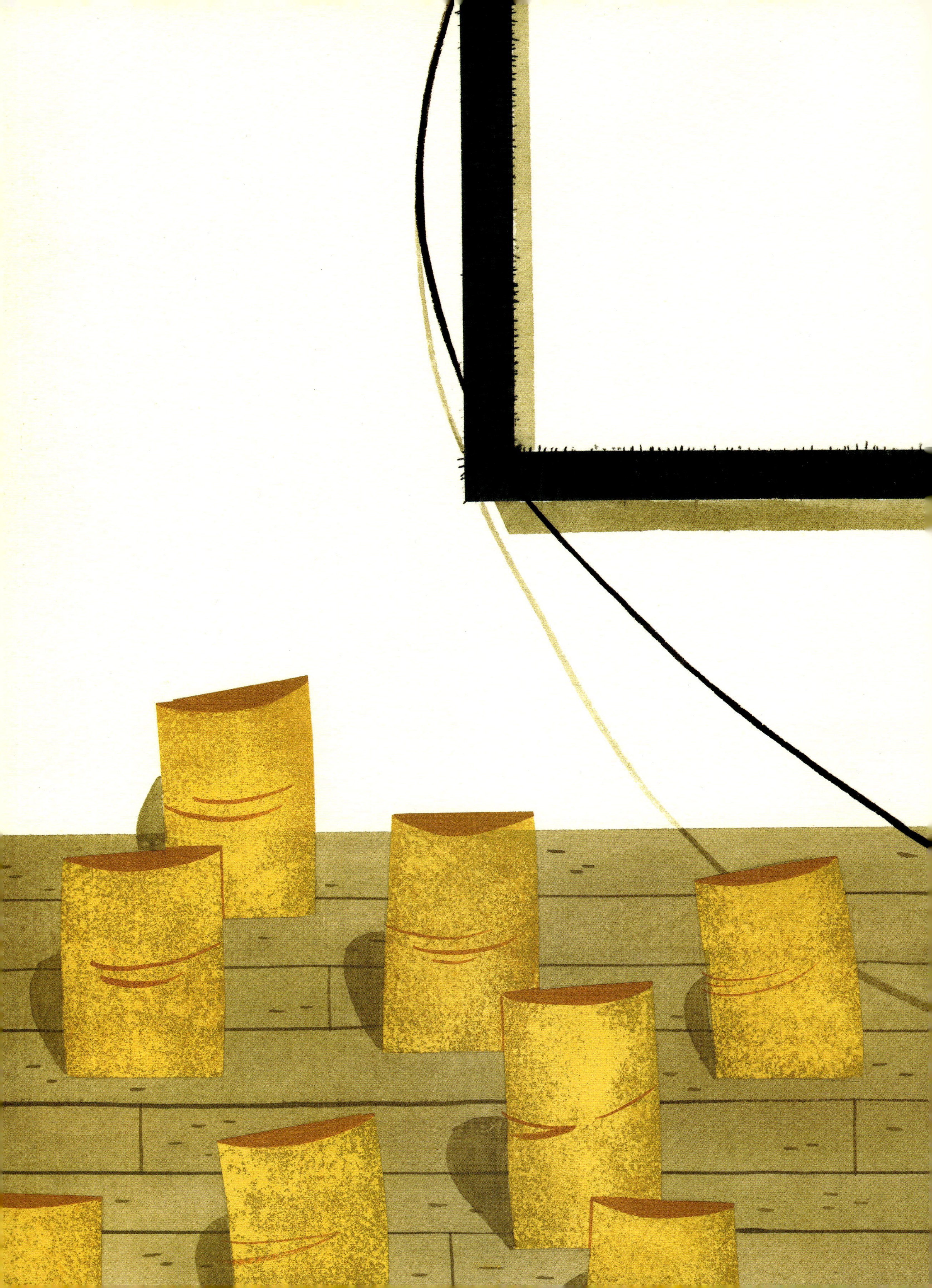

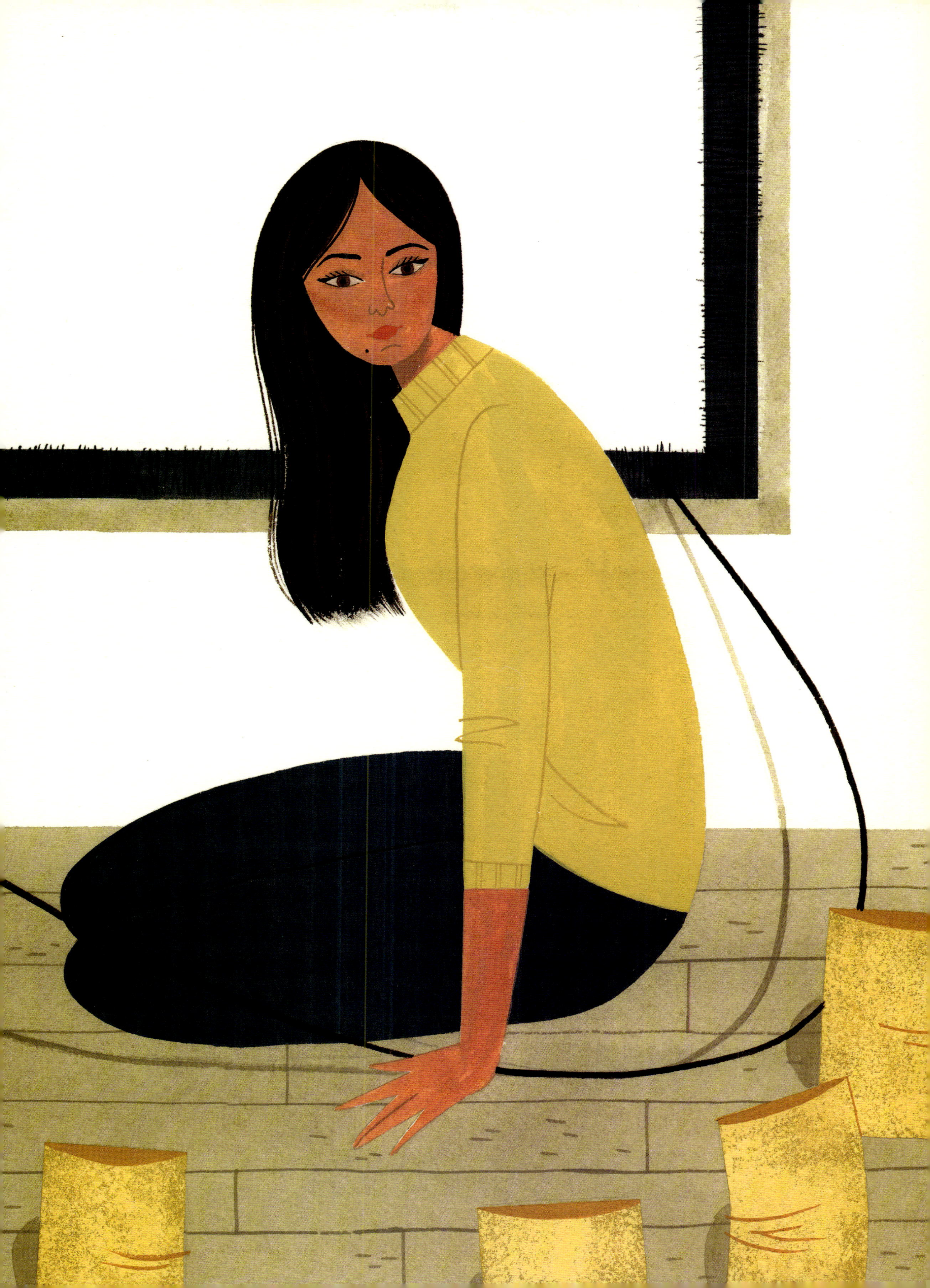

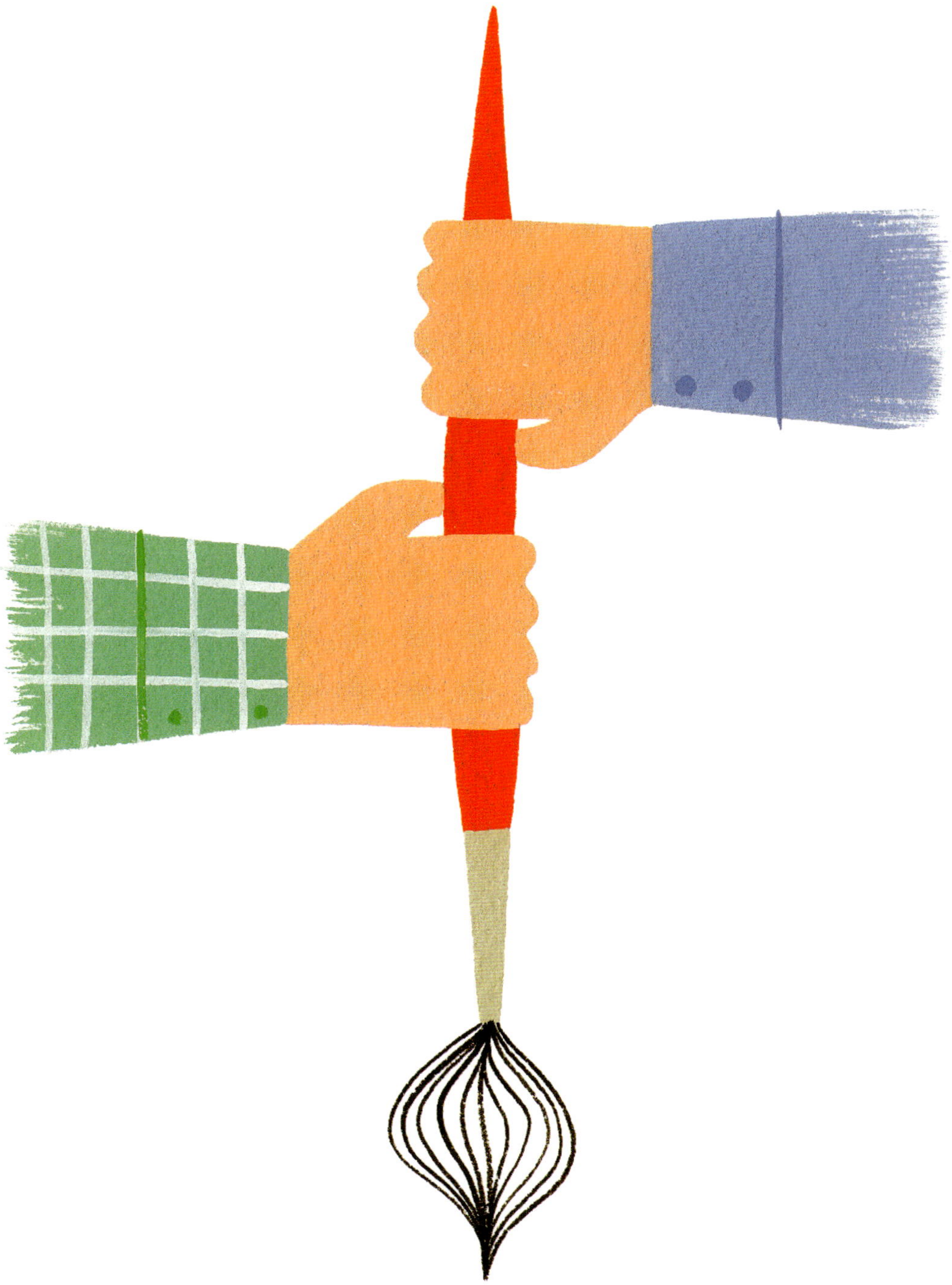

Alice Provensen

“We were a true collaboration. Martin and I really were one artist.”

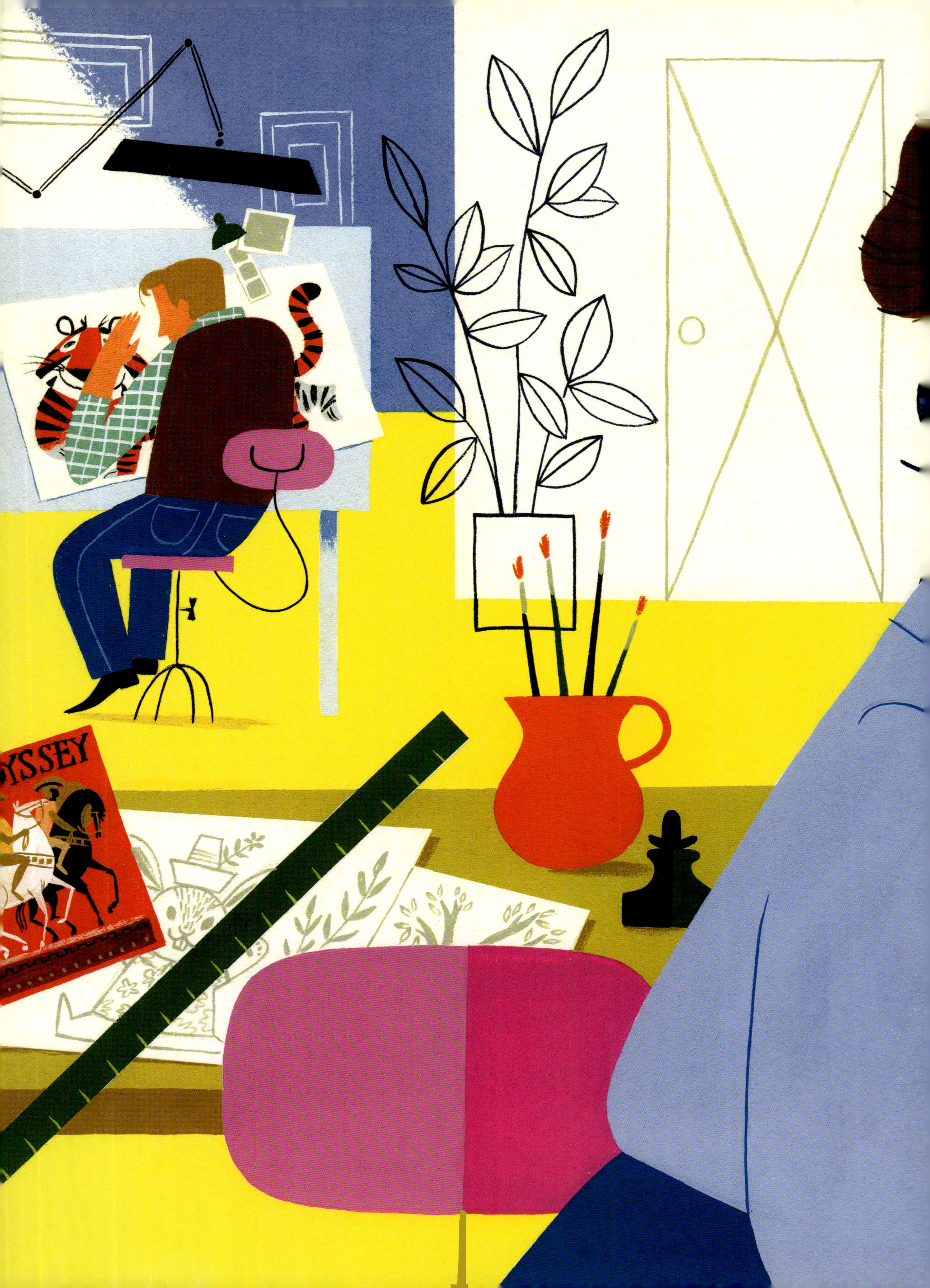
YSSEY

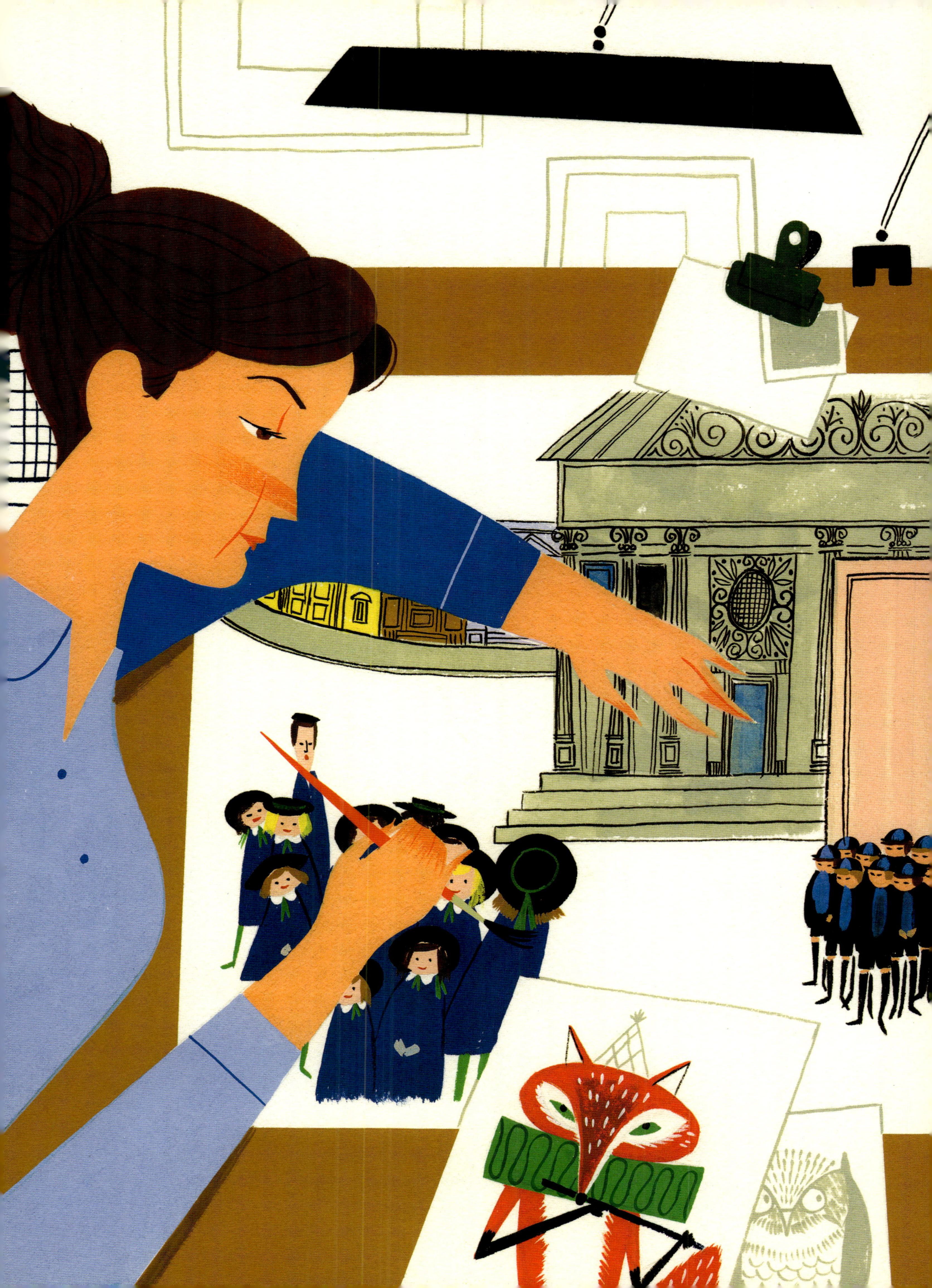

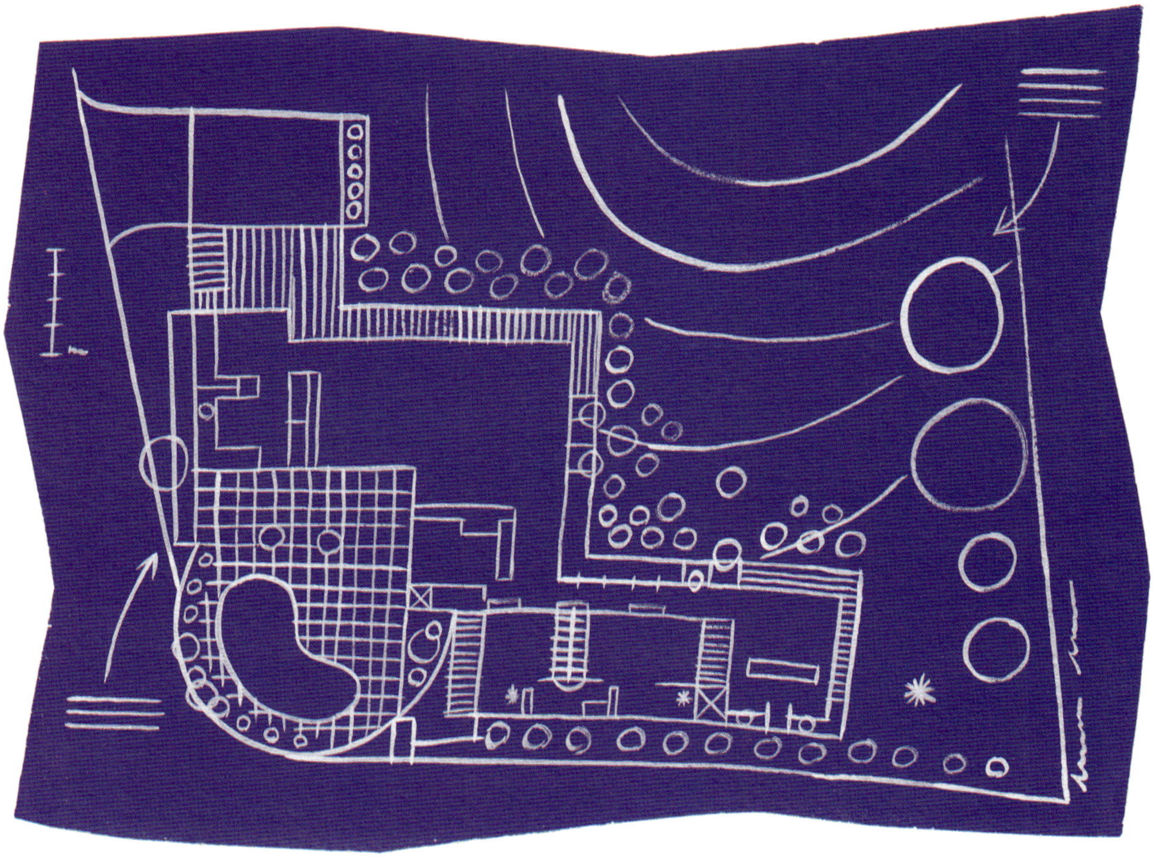

Greta Magnusson-Grossman

"The easiest way to show what you can do is to do it on your own."

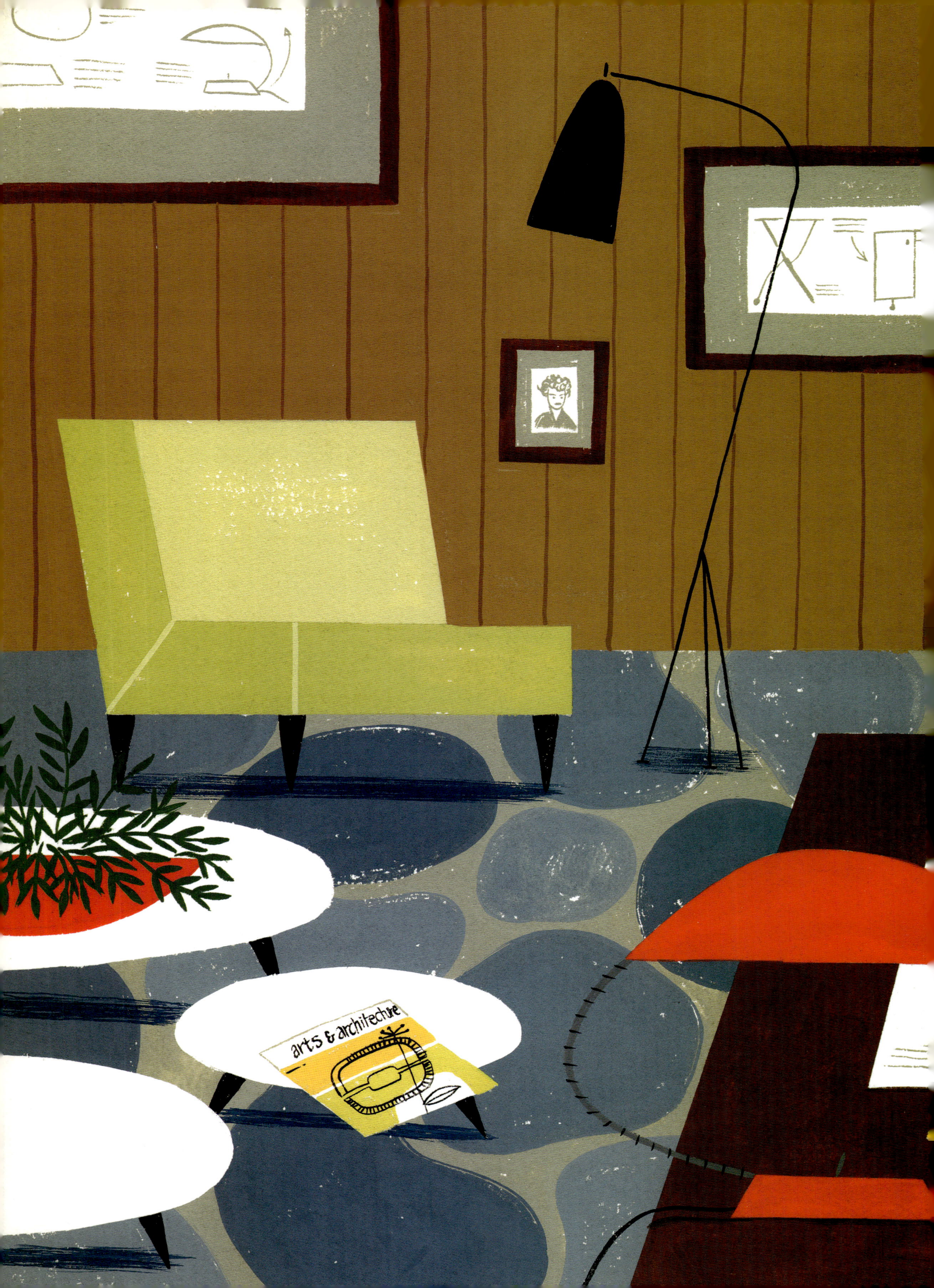
arts & architecture

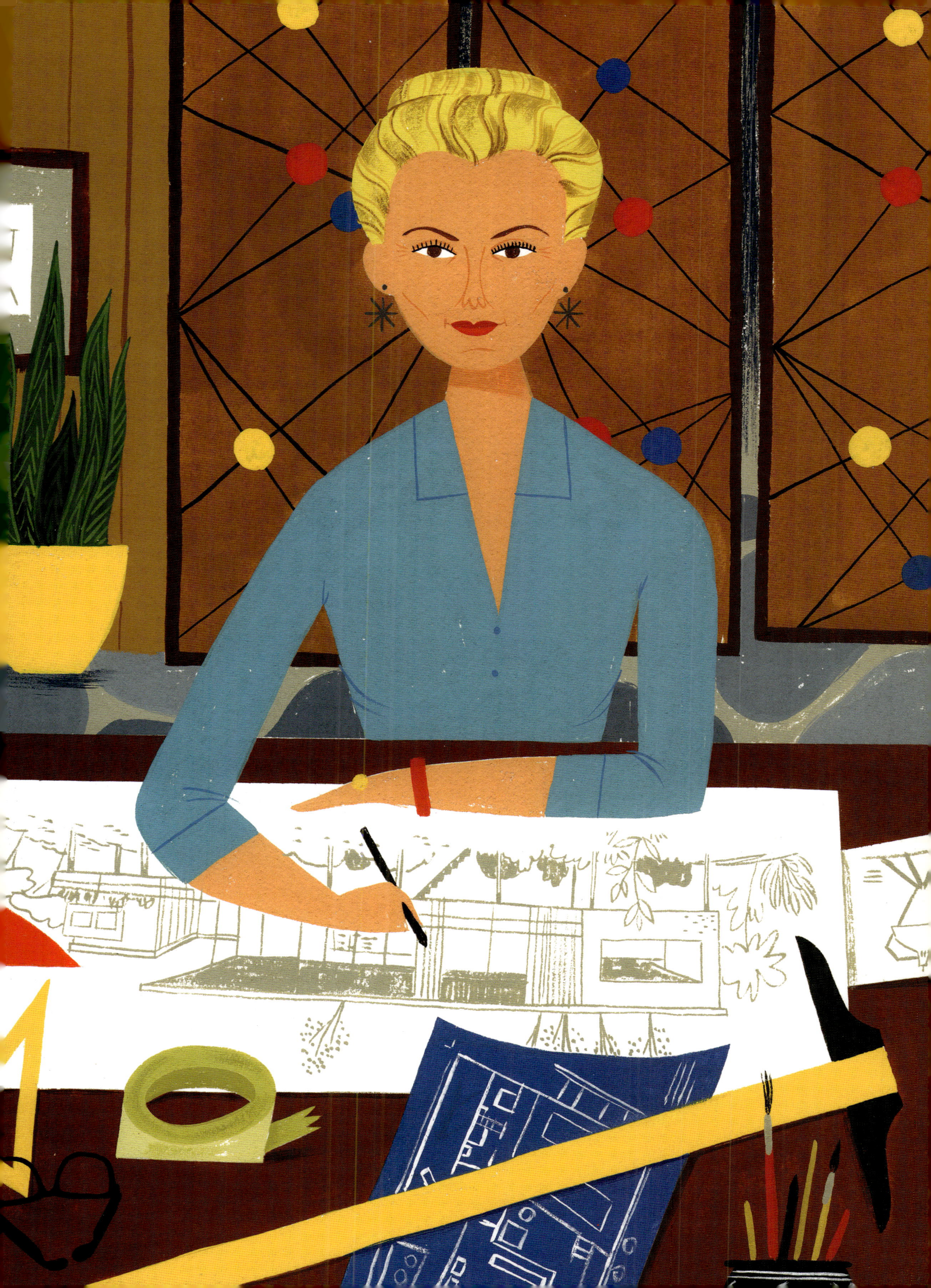

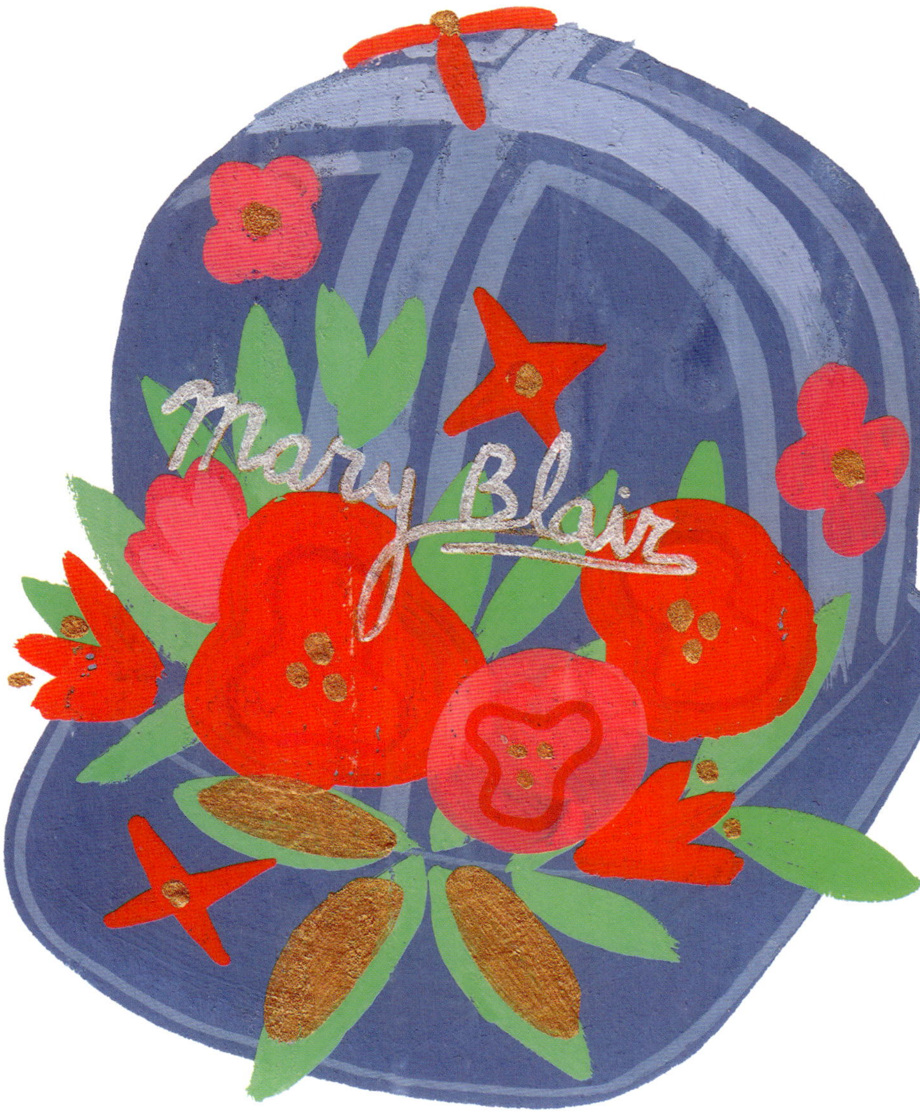

Mary Blair

"Walt [Disney] said that I knew about colors he had never heard of before."

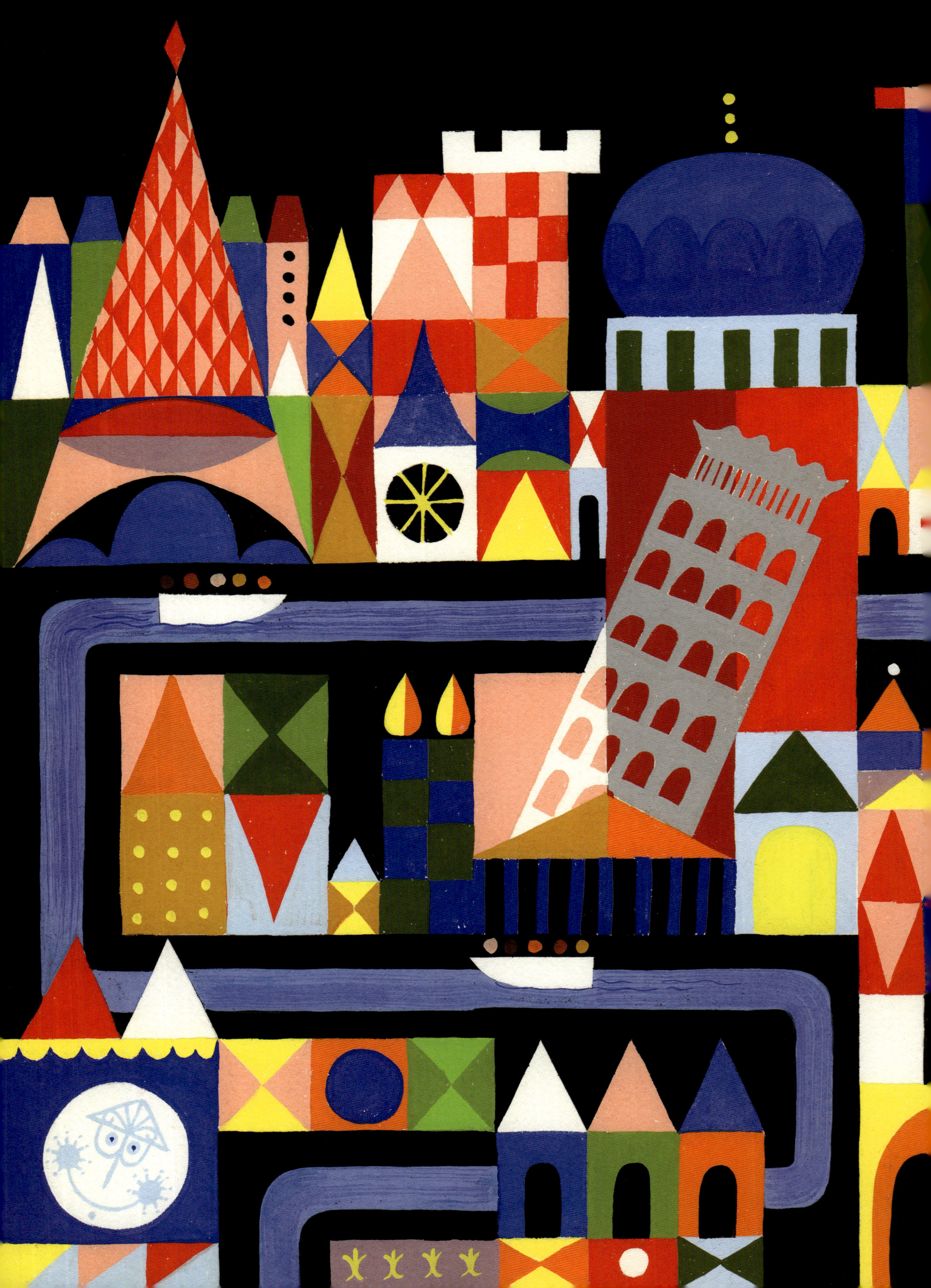

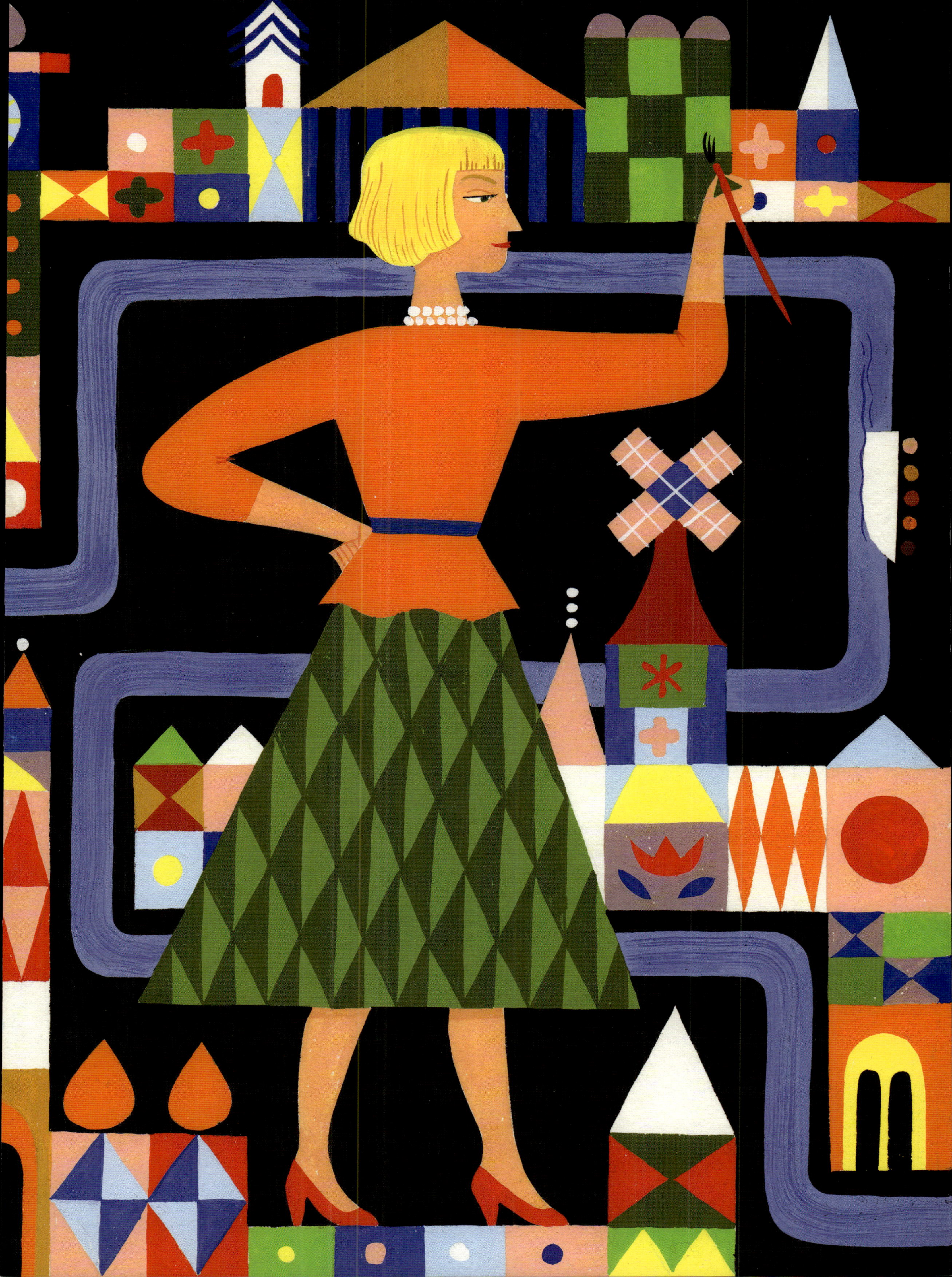

Biographies

1 ***Ray Eames*** (12.15.1912–08.21.1988)

Ray Eames was an artist, designer, and filmmaker most well known for the collaborative work she created with her husband, Charles Eames, and the Eames Office. Ray studied painting with the Abstract Expressionist artist Hans Hoffman in New York, and studied design at the Cranbrook Academy of Art in Michigan. At Cranbrook, Ray delved into many creative pursuits, foreshadowing the multi-disciplinary work of the Eames Office. As Ray later said, "I never gave up painting, I just changed my palette." It was also at Cranbrook that Ray met Charles, and within a year, in 1941, the two were married. The Eameses then moved west and set up the Eames Office in Venice, California, producing some of the most seminal furniture designs of the twentieth century, including Ray's sculptural, walnut stools for the Time-Life building that are still manufactured by Herman Miller to this day. During this time, Ray also designed many covers for the very influential *Arts & Architecture* magazine, created textile designs that are still produced by Maharam, and collaborated with Charles on numerous exhibits, films, toys, and more. In 1949, together they created the Case Study House #8, the landmark mid-twentieth-century residence that was to become their home for the rest of their lives. Ray meticulously displayed her folk art collection and treasures from their travels throughout their home. Far from the starkness that many associate with Modernism, the Eameses' home was, and still is, a space filled with warmth, personality, and delightful details curated by Ray Eames. Underscoring their lifelong partnership and connection to each other, Ray passed away ten years to the day that Charles died.

2 ***Edith Head*** (10.28.1897–10.24.1981)

Edith Head is probably the most well-known costume designer in Hollywood, even to this day. She was nominated for thirty-five Academy Awards, including every year from 1948 through 1966, and won eight times—more Oscars than any other woman. Despite earning degrees in French and Romance Languages from UC Berkeley and Stanford universities in Northern California, Edith Head was completely self-taught in the field of costume design. At Paramount Pictures in Hollywood, she quickly became a favorite of movie stars and directors, and created memorable costumes for Grace Kelly in Alfred Hitchcock's *To Catch a Thief*, as well as Audrey Hepburn's quintessential look in *Breakfast at Tiffany's*, to name just a few. Unlike her male contemporaries, Edith was known for consulting with her female stars extensively. It was because of this practice that she became a favorite amongst some of the biggest leading ladies in Hollywood. There were even a few stars for whom she designed a personal wardrobe. One of those stars was Barbara Stanwyck, whose son Dion secretly offered Edith $6 to make a "nice dress" for his mommy's Christmas present. When Edith agreed, Stanwyck supplied the remaining several hundred dollars. When Edith was asked about her favorite star to dress, she said, "I've dressed thousands of actors, actresses, and animals, but whenever I am asked which star is my personal favorite, I answer, 'Grace Kelly.' She is a charming lady, a most gifted actress, and, to me, a valued friend." With her signature bangs, thick-rimmed, round glasses, and tailored two-piece suits, Edith Head's personal style was a serious and consistent uniform that was in stark contrast to her elaborate and feminine designs.

3 ***Peggy Moffitt*** (b. 05.14.1940)

During the 1960s, the California born-and-raised model Peggy Moffitt caused a sensation as the muse for both fashion designer Rudi Gernreich's bold and graphic clothing designs, and her photographer husband William Claxton's classic and stunning photographs of Peggy in these designs. Perhaps none more so than Gernreich's monokini. The monokini was a bathing suit that revealed a woman's top half and was a symbol of the freedom and liberation that was emerging around that period of time. The striking black-and-white photograph of Peggy modeling the monokini was taken by her renowned photographer husband, whose images immortalized the likes of Jazz legend Chet Baker, film star Steve McQueen, and so many other notable artists of the era. It became a worldwide news event when *Women's Wear Daily* published the photograph in 1964, catapulting Peggy into the media spotlight. Peggy's background in dance gave a fluidity to her movements that was captured on film by William Claxton. Together they created what is considered the first fashion video: *Basic Black*, which is now in the permanent collection at MoMA in New York. Additionally, in 1966, Peggy appeared alongside Vanessa Redgrave and Veruschka in italian director Michelangelo Antonioni's cult classic *Blow Up*, a film that captured the zeitgeist of the the swinging sixties in London through the lens of a fashion photographer. Coupled with her Kabuki-style makeup she created herself and her five-point, geometric Vidal Sassoon haircut, Peggy invented a look all her own. Indeed, she wasn't just a model; she was also an aesthetic collaborator and communicator whose signature visual style helped define an era.

4 ***Yayoi Kusama*** (b. 03.22.1929)

Straying from tradition all of her life, Yayoi Kusama has flourished with an artistic career based largely on her obsession with polka dots. As a young girl in Japan, her parents did not support her creative pursuits, so Yayoi used sacks from the family's plant business as painting canvas. Even as she began her training at the Kyoto Art Academy, Yayoi rejected the school's traditional teachings and began to infuse her now-famous polka dots into her artwork. Over the course of her lifetime, Yayoi has endured effects of mental illness, including hallucinations, but rather than be burdened by these experiences, she has used them as inspiration, and her artwork as an escape. In fact, since the 1970s, Yayoi has voluntarily lived in a mental hospital in Japan a short distance away from her studio. Despite this unusual setup, or more likely because of it, Yayoi has emerged as one of the most prolific and recognized artists of our time. Beginning in the 1950s and 1960s, Yayoi began painting surfaces with her now-signature polka dots. She has created paintings, performance art pieces, and installations, including her amazing and immersive *Infinity Mirrored* rooms that have become celebrated, must-see events in world-class museums around the world. Yayoi has had recent retrospective shows at both the Museum of Modern Art and the Whitney Museum of American Art in New York, as well as the Tate Modern in London. And at eighty-six years young, she continues to create new pieces, and work with her beloved polka dots: "Polka dots can't stay alone. When we obliterate nature and our bodies with polka dots we become part of the unity of our environments."

5 ***Frida Kahlo*** (07.06.1907–07.13.1954)

One of the most important artists of the twentieth century, Frida Kahlo is known for her striking appearance, her turbulent marriage to painter Diego Rivera, and her vibrant paintings. Frida often incorporated the lush colors, vegetation, and wildlife of her native Mexico, and her self-portraits often depicted references to the body and physical pain and injury, a reference to a childhood of polio and a debilitating bus accident at the age of eighteen. Frida is quoted as saying, "I paint myself because I am so often alone, and because I am the subject I know best." Despite experiencing such physical pain, she forged a life and a career on her own terms and was openly bisexual in a time and a culture where this was taboo. Frida received her first solo exhibition in 1938 in New York City at the Julien Levy Gallery. From there she began to receive further recognition for her artwork, traveling to Paris and befriending Pablo Picasso. After returning to Mexico, Frida continued to paint, as well as teaching art and becoming a member of the Seminario de Cultura Mexicana—to promote Mexican art and culture. Throughout her life, Frida continued to face health issues, and when she received her first solo exhibition in Mexico in 1953, her doctor forbid her from attending. Too determined to miss such an important event, she was carried on a stretcher and lay on a bed in the center of the gallery. Still, it was not until after Frida's death, at age forty-seven, that her life and her paintings became truly famous and appreciated worldwide.

6 ***Maija Isola*** (03.15.1927–03.03.2001)

Known for her bright, floral and geometric patterns produced for Finnish design house Marimekko, Maija Isola created brilliant textile designs for more than three decades. She began her career at the esteemed company, formerly Printex, in 1949, and during her thirty-eight years with the firm, she designed more than 500 pieces. Maija found inspiration from her travels abroad and was very influenced by folk art, modern visual art, and nature. Often thought of as a recluse, Maija preferred working at home alone, sitting on a sheepskin on the floor, surrounded by her paint and brushes. Maija designed her most well-known pattern, Unikko (Poppy) in 1964, against the wishes of Marimekko founder Armi Ratia, who disliked and forbid floral patterns. Thankfully, since its inception, the pattern has been in continuous production, appearing everywhere from Nordic walking poles to Hong Kong tram cars, a hot air balloon, and everyday objects, including aprons, shower curtains, lunch bags, and tea towels. In the 1980s, Maija began working with her daughter Kristina, who was just three years old when her mother first started her career at Printex. Kristina wrote of her mother's time and legacy as a designer, "When I was a child, Maija would work and take care of me at the same time. She would tell me a story while drawing a textile pattern. ... My mother taught me to be methodical and plan my work beforehand. She would say that it's better to sit and think before you do anything." Maija spent the later years of her life focusing on painting, rather than textile design, harkening back to her time in the 1940s studying art at the Helsinki Art School.

7 *Sister Corita Kent* (11.20.1918–09.18.1986)

Sister Corita Kent was not your average nun. Corita was an icon for the "rebellious modern nun" during the tumultuous 1960s as the head of the art department at the progressively minded Immaculate Heart College in Los Angeles. Encouraged by the social reforms of the day, Sister Corita encouraged her students to look at the world differently by gathering inspiration from the world around them. Sister Corita drew most of her inspiration from billboards, hand-painted signs, and pop culture. During her three-week vacations from school she was known to create anywhere from thirty to thirty-five different silk-screened prints in editions of 100 each. Her work consisted of bright neon colors and typography, which mirrored many different advertising slogans, as well as pop culture references of the time. But what made each print cohesive was the way in which she would alter the meaning of the advertising slogans to no longer reflect a commercial product, but instead to reflect an uplifting message of spirituality. Sister Corita enjoyed a mutual admiration from some of the biggest names in the arts of that period, including Alfred Hitchcock, John Cage, Saul Bass, Buckminster Fuller, and Charles and Ray Eames. She became such a friend of Charles and Ray that she and her students often frequented their studio. By the end of the 1960s, the Immaculate Heart nuns were deemed too radical for the archdiocese in their quest for modest changes and self-governance, ultimately resulting in their decision to leave the Catholic Church altogether. Luckily, Corita continued to paint her optimistic and beautiful hopes for humanity until the end of her life.

8 *Coco Chanel* (08.19.1883–01.10.1971)

Her name conjures up images of haute couture clothing, classic perfume, and pure elegance. She was Coco Chanel: a style inspiration, a fashion pioneer, and a formidable business presence. Known for reinventing herself and her past, certain details of Gabrielle Chanel's young life are a mystery, including when and why she became "Coco" instead of Gabrielle. Despite a childhood in poverty, the loss of her mother when she was just eleven years old, followed by life in an orphanage, Coco overcame her hardships to become the legend we know of today. It was at the orphanage where Coco began learning to sew, followed by more lessons at the Notre Dame school she attended when she turned eighteen. Coco opened her first shop in Paris in 1910, selling hats and then gradually making and selling her own clothing. In the 1920s she created Chanel No. 5 perfume and introduced the firsts in a famous collection of Chanel suits and little black dresses, transforming black from something mournful into a chic evening style: "I imposed black; it's still going strong today, for black wipes out everything else around." Additionally, she also designed costumes for stage productions, and struck up friendships and romances with notable figures like Igor Stravinsky. The 1930s brought economic hardship, and Coco was forced to close her business for some time. But in 1953, at the age of seventy, Coco relaunched her fashion career—and the House of Chanel continues to thrive today, more than forty years after her death. Her legacy lives on, perhaps just as she predicted: "May my legend prosper and thrive. I wish it a long and happy life."

9 *Bridget Riley* (b. 04.24.1931)

Bridget Riley is known for her graphic, bold, geometric Op Art paintings that she began creating in the 1960s, quickly rising to fame as a young artist still in her thirties. Bridget had studied at the Royal College of Art in London, but her time there was a struggle, as she desired to develop her own style. Eventually Bridget discovered the work of Abstract Expressionist painters, and she began to experiment with new directions. In the early 1960s, while teaching and studying at London's Hornsey College of Art, Bridget explored a new area: painting geometric shapes in black and white—her first Op Art paintings. This series of works would launch her career on a new path; she began to receive significant recognition for pieces like *Movement in Squares* (1961) and *Where* (1964). These paintings often tricked the eye, and their graphic visuals became iconically linked to the hallucinatory and pop-art aesthetics of the era. Bridget's solid standing in the Op Art movement made her a celebrity in Great Britain's art world. Of her process for creating art, she said, "In the early 1960s I realized that the most exciting way of setting about work was to establish limits, in terms of each particular piece, which would sometimes push me and the work as we evolved together into such tight corners that they yielded surprising riches. ... Through limiting oneself, even severely, one discovers things that one would never have dreamt of." Bridget eventually brought color into her work, and expanded in other areas as well, including murals and ballet set design. Now in her eighties, Bridget continues to create as her work has become even more revered.

10 *Ruth Asawa* (01.24.1926–08.05.2013)

Born to Japanese parents, with six brothers and sisters, Ruth (Aiko) Asawa was raised on a vegetable farm in California during the Great Depression. Following the attack on Pearl Harbor in 1941, the family was forced from their homes into internment, first at horse stables at the racetrack in Santa Anita, California. A few Japanese artists from Disney Studios were also interned there and were the first to teach Ruth how to draw. Ruth's family was transferred to an internment camp in Arkansas, where she finished high school, earning her admission to attend the Milwaukee State Teachers College. There she took every art course offered but ultimately was unable to graduate when no school in Wisconsin would hire a Japanese-American woman to complete her student teaching requirement. Afterwards, Ruth attended Black Mountain College in North Carolina, where she met her husband, architect and designer Albert Lanier. Staying home to raise their children, Ruth began to sculpt, working on a wire piece she had started at Black Mountain. She was inspired to use wire after a visit to Mexico, where she observed baskets in the markets for eggs and produce: "My materials were simple, and whenever there was a free moment, I would sit down and do some work."Ruth became known for her weaved, wire sculptures, as well as her public fountain installations throughout San Francisco. She co-founded a public school for the arts in 1982, now known as the Ruth Asawa San Francisco School of the Arts; and in 1998, the University of Wisconsin-Milwaukee, previously the Milwaukee State Teachers College, awarded Ruth the bachelor's degree she had been prevented from earning so many years before.

11 *Twiggy* (b. 09.19.1949)

Known for her slender frame, giant eyes, and blond bob, Twiggy and her distinct, androgynous look became a sensation in the 1960s and '70s in London's mod scene—earning her the groundbreaking title of the first international supermodel. Unlike the curvaceous, full-figured, and overtly sexualized models of the 1950s, Twiggy's look was nonconformist, boyish, and thoroughly modern. Twiggy modeled many of British fashion designer Mary Quant's clothes, and her look became synonymous with the designer's famed miniskirts. Born Lesley Hornby, the stunning Twiggy received her iconic nickname at the beginning of her career, as a thin teenager with long limbs growing up in England. And it wasn't long before her name was known in households worldwide. Twiggy's popularity was instant, as she appeared on the covers of successful fashion magazines, including *Elle* and *British Vogue*, working with established photographers like Richard Avedon. Her images defined the era, and she became an idol and inspiration for young women across the globe. Using her fame to her business advantage, Twiggy branched out to create a clothing line, began acting on the stage and screen, and inspired consumer products, including a Barbie doll, lunch box, and board game. For her performance in the stage production *My One and Only* she earned a Tony nomination, and as Polly Browne in the film *The Boy Friend*, she received two Golden Globe awards. In recent years, Twiggy has served as an animal activist and supporter of breast cancer research groups. And her striking appearance and cheeky personality have granted Twiggy an iconic and lasting presence in the annals of fashion.

12 *Mary Quant* (b. 02.11.1934)

Bold, graphic, colorful, and patterned, Mary Quant's fashion designs were synonymous with the Mod aesthetics of the 1960s. She may not have invented the minidress, but Mary Quant brought fame and recognition to the fashionable style, even wearing a minidress herself to accept an OBE from the Queen of England in 1966. International supermodel Twiggy wore the style frequently, and the girls who came into Mary's Chelsea shop asked for their hems to be shorter and shorter. But this garment wasn't her only contribution to the fashion industry; with her signature Vidal Sassoon bob and plastic boots, she modeled and marketed her own innovations—from her shop, Bazaar, in London to her tour through America. Her youthful lines appealed to a large demographic, and J.C. Penney purchased 6,000 of her garments in the early 1960s. Her carefully arranged shop windows in Bazaar drew in interest and customers, and the rise in popularity allowed Mary to open a second branch of her store in 1963. Success continued, including a hot pants trend, and Mary later launched the Ginger Group to offer her designs to a wide range of consumers at more affordable prices, with her label appearing worldwide on beauty products and accessories as well. In her 1966 autobiography, *Quant by Quant*, she commented on her preference for mass appeal: "What ready-to-wear does today, the couturiers—even the Paris couturiers—confirm tomorrow. It has happened several times already. I think it will go on happening." In the 1960s and '70s Mary added makeup and household goods to her repertoire, even designing the interior of the Mini Designer car in 1988.

13 *Louise Nevelson* (09.23.1899–04.17.1988)

Louise Nevelson is known for her large-scale, collage-like sculptures that house multiple compartments and objects in relief united by a single color. Louise was born in Czarist Russia to a Jewish family in 1899. Her family immigrated to the United States in 1905, and by 1920, Louise was married and living in New York. By 1929 she became a full-time student at the Art Students League. Two years later she traveled to Munich to study with Hans Hofmann, walking by Adolf Hitler's house every day on her way to the school. While in Europe, Louise was influenced by Picasso's Cubism, and was inspired to create her own three-dimensional sculptures, initially in wood, that often incorporated found objects, such as table legs, into her pieces. One of her most important pieces, *Sky Cathedral* (1958), is a large-scale, wooden, interior sculpture painted black, which now lives in the permanent collection of MoMA in New York City. Louise's first solo exhibition occurred in 1941, but it wasn't until almost reaching sixty that her body of work earned the respect and recognition she'd struggled for over decades. In her seventies, Louise began working on even larger-scale outdoor sculptures and utilized Corten steel. Beyond her larger-than-life sculptures, Louise's personality was much the same—she was known as strong, flamboyant, bisexual, and striking, with a penchant for false eyelashes and vibrant scarves. Of her single-minded pursuit of art creation she said, "I never got caught [up] in making a living. That would have seemed to be a little bit out of order to a creative mind such as mine."

14 *Elaine Lustig Cohen* (b. 03.06.1927)

A recipient of the distinguished American Institute of Graphic Arts medal in 2011, Elaine Lustig Cohen has earned a reputation as a talented graphic designer and artist over the past eighty-eight years. Growing up in New Jersey, Elaine's mother instilled in her a sense that she could accomplish anything of interest, no matter her gender. Elaine took drawing lessons and eventually earned a bachelor's degree in fine arts. In 1948 she married designer Alvin Lustig, and the two were together for seven years, until Alvin's untimely death at age forty. During their marriage Elaine worked as an assistant to Alvin, who owned his own Manhattan design firm. Upon Alvin's death, it became Elaine's responsibility to fill her husband's shoes. Thus at age twenty-eight, with no formal graphic design training, Elaine took the reins and proved herself a talented designer in her own right. Architect Phillip Johnson commissioned her to design the signage for the Seagram Building. Eventually, she began to specialize in signage, book jacket design, catalogs, and other pursuits. Alvin had designed twenty-five book covers for Meridian Books, and Elaine went on to design more than a hundred. At this time she was one of very few women to own and run her own high-profile graphic design firm. Throughout her life Elaine has continued to change and evolve, and she continues to explore new avenues of design, including printmaking and digital work. In a 2013 interview, she spoke about her artistic methods: "The wonderful thing about being an artist is you never know exactly where you are going with a process. ... You're always opening another door and finding something unexpected."

15 *Helen Frankenthaler* (12.12.1928–12.27.2011)

Helen Frankenthaler was one of the foremost painters of the mid-twentieth century. Early in her career, Helen was influenced by many of the major artists of Abstract Expressionism she was fortunate enough to meet, including Jackson Pollock, Franz Kline, and Robert Motherwell—whom she went on to marry. Helen had a privileged upbringing that garnered many opportunities that helped shape her artistic voice. While still in high school at Dalton she studied with Mexican painter Rufino Tamayo, and later at Bennington College she studied with Paul Feeley. Helen developed her own method of painting referred to as the "soak-stain" technique, where she would pour turpentine-thinned oil paint onto oversized canvases, creating large, luminescent areas of color. This breakthrough was hailed by critics and seen as an instrumental part of what was called the new Color Field movement. Helen often found inspiration for her works in landscapes of nature, as was the case for *Mountains and Sea* (1952), which she painted after returning home from a trip to Nova Scotia. As an abstract artist, her focus was not on literal interpretation of her subject matter: "What concerns me when I work is not whether the picture is a landscape, or whether it's pastoral, or whether somebody will see a sunset in it. What concerns me is: did I make a beautiful picture?" Both Helen and Robert came from well-to-do families and were known to live a lavish lifestyle; they were fond of entertaining at their home on the Upper East side of New York. In New York, Helen's work is part of the permanent collections at MoMA and the Guggenheim, as well as many more museums around the world.

16 *Eva Zeisel* (11.13.1906–12.30.2011)

A prolific and accomplished modern designer, Eva Zeisel lived a remarkable and long life. She was falsely imprisoned in the 1930s for plotting against Joseph Stalin, and she narrowly escaped the German army in 1938, leaving Vienna for America: "I saw the Statue of Liberty and my fears came down. It was a very touching reception." When Eva was a child, her mother, Laura, opened a progressive kindergarten, where Eva learned about art, music, and movement. Her parents emphasized playfulness in her early life, and certainly encouraged her creativity. During her time at the Budapest Royal Academy of Fine Arts, her mother suggested that she switch from painting to a more practical career in ceramics—a path that would ultimately lead her to great success. As soon as she moved to the United States, Eva began receiving ceramics commissions, as well as becoming the first person to teach ceramics as industrial design for mass production at the Pratt Institute. Eva believed in producing quality products at an affordable price for many people to enjoy and appreciate. Living to 105 years old, Eva continued to design even after her centennial birthday. Upon her death, *The New York Times* wrote of Eva as "a ceramic artist whose elegant, eccentric designs for dinnerware in the 1940s and '50s helped to revolutionize the way Americans set their tables. ... [She] brought the clean, casual shapes of modernist design into middle-class American homes with furnishings that encouraged a postwar desire for fresh, less formal styles of living." Indeed, after a career that spanned over eighty years, Eva's sculptural and distinctive dinnerware is still commercially available to this day.

17 *Georgia O'Keeffe* (11.15.1887–03.06.1986)

American painter Georgia O'Keeffe found inspiration in nature, focusing on various regions of the United States. From a young age, she enjoyed spending time outdoors, touching and feeling everything on her family's Wisconsin farm. Her mother instilled in her a love of art, and Georgia pursued further art education as she grew up. She went on to teach art in Texas before famed photographer Alfred Stieglitz invited her to New York to paint. After working together for some time, the two were married in 1924, and moved into a high-rise hotel in the city, where Georgia could paint views of the sprawling metropolis. Alfred had a summer home in Lake George, New York, as well, and there Georgia drew from the rural setting for her work in the 1920s. Her paintings covered a varied range of subjects, including abstract views, brightly colored flowers, and the New Mexico desert, where she traveled frequently. She used bleached animal bones from that area as subject matter for her artworks, pairing them with foliage and other landscapes. Her paintings rarely featured people or animals, but rather focused on natural objects, including flowers, seashells, clouds, or simply shapes she imagined in her mind's eye. Following her husband's death in 1946, Georgia settled in New Mexico permanently—there she felt the blue skies and desert flowers, among other elements, best served her work. During her ninety-eights years, Georgia also lobbied for women's equal rights for several decades, even telling Eleanor Roosevelt that she "would like each child to feel ... that no door for any activity that they may choose is closed on account of sex."

18 *Florence Knoll* (b. 05.24.1917)

Born of German ancestry and raised in Michigan, Florence Knoll found an interest in architecture and design early in life, at the Kingswood School for Girls. At the Cranbrook Academy of Art next door, Florence met and eventually studied under architect Eliel Saarinen, later becoming close friends with Eliel's son, an architect and designer in his own right, Eero Saarinen. Florence continued her education and studied under a host of esteemed industry figures, including renowned architect and the head of the Bauhaus school Mies van de Rohe, whose "less is more" philosophy she noted as having "a profound effect on my design approach and the clarification of design." Upon her move to New York City in 1941, Florence met (and eventually married) furniture designer Hans Knoll, and the two grew the Knoll company into an internationally respected success. Florence herself pioneered the Knoll Planning Unit, which provided modern, efficient interior design for corporate offices, depending on the needs of each individual client. In addition, she provided what she called the "meat and potatoes" of Knoll Associates' furniture offerings, in contrast to the more specialized pieces that were created by revered outside designers and by others within the company. Her own designs may have seemed like basics to her, but they are now considered Modernist classics in their own right. Following the untimely death of Hans in 1955, Florence took over as president of the company. As an architect, interior designer, industrial designer, and business woman, Florence helmed one of the most esteemed and successful furniture businesses in America. More than half a century later, Florence Knoll and the business she created are still going strong.

19 ***Edith Heath*** (05.24.1911–12.27.2005)

The founder of the esteemed Heath Ceramics, Edith Heath was born and raised on a family farm near Sioux City, Iowa. The daughter of a headstrong mother, Edith learned to diligently pursue her own interests, a trait that served her well later in life. She took her first ceramics class at the Art Institute of Chicago. In 1938 she married Brian Heath and traveled through New Mexico, where she encountered the work of a famous Native American potter, later saying, "We visited a pueblo and I fell in love with the ceramic work of Maria Martinez. Although I had little training in ceramics, I decided then, 'this is what I want to do.'" She began teaching art in San Francisco, and after converting her laundry room into a studio, Edith experimented with various materials and techniques, and began creating dishes and vases. Soon Edith was creating pieces for the well-known retailer Gump's. In 1948, Heath Ceramics was founded after Edith exhibited a solo pottery show at San Francisco's Legion of Honor. As her company grew and production was streamlined, Edith observed: "Good design doesn't depend on whether something is made by hand. In fact, there are some very junky things that can be made by hand. ... It was okay while I was learning and getting a feel for the clay. But after all, a machine doesn't decide what the shape is going to be. A human being has to decide that ... so I felt I was in as much control as ever." By 1949, Heath Ceramics was producing 100,000 pieces a year, and the Sausalito, California-based company continues to thrive today more than half a century later.

20 ***Alma Thomas*** (09.22.1891–02.24.1978)

Alma Thomas was born in Columbus, Georgia, in 1891, but her family was forced to relocate to Washington, D.C. in 1906 to flee racial violence in the South. As a girl growing up she had dreamed of becoming an architect, which was seemingly impossible at the time, but instead graduated from Howard University with a degree in fine arts in the 1920s, becoming the first graduate of the university's art department. She also studied at Columbia and New York universities in the 1930s. Alma Thomas went on to have a thirty-five-year career teaching art at Shaw Junior High School in Washington, D.C., often bringing her students to art exhibits at the Smithsonian Institution. Upon her retirement in 1960, at the age of sixty-eight, she embarked on her fine art career while the civil rights movement was still in its infancy. Influenced by Abstract Expressionism she created her own beautiful Color Field paintings, developing a bold, multi-hued, mosaic-like technique. But it wasn't until 1972, when Alma was more than eighty years old, that she was fully recognized for her own artistic contributions, after being "discovered" by the Whitney Museum of American Art and awarded their first solo exhibition of an African-American woman's artworks. In the last years of her life, esteem for Alma only grew, with September 9th declared Alma W. Thomas day in our nation's capital in 1972, and an invitation from President Jimmy Carter to visit the White House in 1977. Recently, President Obama and First Lady Michelle Obama proudly unveiled an Alma Thomas painting at the White House, the first artwork by an African-American woman to be featured there.

21 ***Vera Neumann*** (07.24.1907–6.15.1993)

Vera Neumann created wearable art with her stylish scarves, elegant designs, and recognizable ladybug logo. Creating a brand based on her own original artworks, this entrepreneur thrived for decades, with pieces appearing virtually everywhere throughout the 1960s. Vera found art at a young age in the meadows and woods near her Stamford, Connecticut, home. Her father encouraged her passion, and he took her weekly to the Metropolitan Museum of Art, as well as hiring a sign painter to give her art lessons. She attended The Cooper Union for the Advancement of Science and Art and the Traphagen School of Design, where she learned about the potential for developing her creativity into a viable career and business. During this time, Vera began to illustrate children's books, design textiles, and create murals for children's rooms. After marrying George Neumann, Vera and her new husband formed a creative partnership, and he suggested she create fabrics from her vibrant paintings. From there they launched a successful business of many years, producing placemats and napkins, aprons and pot holders, dish towels and bed sheets, not to mention brilliant fabrics and her exquisite scarf collections. In the 1960s, Vera expanded to clothing lines, with celebrities wearing her designs in magazines and Marilyn Monroe collecting Vera's scarves. In fact, by the 1970s, what started out as a kitchen table business had grown to a $100 million international business. Vera's art and entrepreneurship succeeded in delighting a wide audience. Later in life Vera summed up an inspirational career to *The Washington Post* with a spot-on sentiment: "The creative part of the business is like a fountain; it keeps going, going, going. I never repeat myself."

22 *Eva Hesse* (01.11.1936-05.29.70)

In Eva Hesse's brief thirty-four years of life she suffered and survived through many seemingly insurmountable circumstances. Born in 1936 to an observant Jewish family, Eva and her family escaped Nazi Germany and ultimately immigrated to New York. When Eva was ten years old, her mother committed suicide. Despite these traumatic events in her childhood, Eva pursued her passion for art, studying at The Cooper Union for the Advancement of Science and Art, as well as with Josef Albers at Yale University. Eva began her career in the 1950s as a painter, and then moved into sculpture as well in the next decade. Eva is known for pieces like *Hang Up*: a mixed media Minimalist sculpture about which she said, "It has a kind of depth I don't always achieve and that is a kind of depth or soul or absurdity or life or meaning or feeling or intellect that I want to get. ... It is the most ridiculous structure I have ever made and that is why it is really good." She was a contemporary of minimalist artists Sol LeWitt and Donald Judd. But unlike the rigidity of much of these minimalists artists' works, Eva brought a handmade, organic, and almost sensual quality to her sculpture that emanated from her innovative use of materials. By using latex and fiberglass, Eva Hesse created series of slightly irregular yet repetitive forms in her compelling installations. In a career spanning just ten years before she succumbed to cancer, Eva Hesse's soulful and ephemeral work continues to inspire. In response to comments of the fragility of her work, Eva once said "Life doesn't last; art doesn't last."

23 *Alice Provensen* (b. 08.14.1918)

Encouraged at a young age by her mother and sixth-grade teacher, Alice Provensen always had art supplies at the ready for her childhood creations. When her teacher entered Alice's picture into a contest, she won a scholarship to the Chicago Art Institute's program for public school children, and she's been drawing ever since—encouraging other youngsters to do the same: "Young children make marvelous pictures. There is nothing they can't draw. They paint and draw from their imaginations and the world around them. And they are not afraid to draw anything." As men left to fight in World War II, Alice was able to secure an animator position at Walter Lantz Studios, working on Woody Woodpecker cartoons. She met her future husband, Martin Provensen, and the two moved from Los Angeles to Washington, D.C. They began to work together to illustrate children's books, earning contracts for Golden Books like *The Fuzzy Duckling*; and their careers flourished. Together they created Kellogg's beloved Tony the Tiger. After a few years, the Provensens moved to a farm in the Hudson River Valley and began creating their own books. Eight of their titles earned placement on *The New York Times* list of the Ten Best Illustrated Books of the year, and they earned a Caldecott Medal in 1984. After Martin's death in 1987, Alice eventually returned to her studio to begin illustrating again. Even into her nineties, Alice has continued to develop new ideas for children's books. At ninety-one, she earned a lifetime achievement award from the Eric Carle Museum of Picture Book Art and commented, "Let's face it, it's not a jab in the eye with a stick!"

24 *Greta Magnusson-Grossman* (07.21.1906-08.28.1999)

With varied talents and a proven reputation for quality, Swedish-born Greta Magnusson-Grossman enjoyed a prolific career of more than four decades as a designer and architect living and working first in Europe and then in Los Angeles. As a young adult just starting out, Greta completed a one year woodworking apprenticeship and earned a scholarship to attend the Stockholm arts institution Konstfack, where she learned furniture, ceramics, and textiles design. She received an award for furniture design in 1933, and the same year she opened Studio, a store and workshop, with a Konstfack classmate. With Studio, Greta earned interior and furniture design commissions, including designing a crib for Sweden's Princess Birgitta. Greta immigrated to Los Angeles with her bandleader husband, Billy Grossman, in 1940, and opened her own design shop in Beverly Hills. Her "Swedish modern furniture, rugs, lamps, and other home furnishings" attracted celebrity and industry clients, including Greta Garbo and Gracie Allen. For Barker Brothers' Modern Shop, in the late 1940s, she designed lamps with flexible arms, which were included in the "Good Design" exhibition at MoMA in New York City. During the next ten years, she designed fourteen homes in California and Sweden, many of which have been featured in *Arts & Architecture* magazine, including several still standing today. Of her experience working in Los Angeles, she is known as saying, "[California design] is not a superimposed style, but an answer to present conditions. ... It has developed out of our own preferences for living in a modern way." Greta's work has been featured in countless exhibitions, and in the 1950s, she taught industrial design at UCLA and the Art Center College of Design.

25

Mary Blair (10.21.1911–07.26.1978)

Mary Blair was inspired to become an illustrator by Pruett Carter, an illustrator and professor of hers at the renowned Chouinard Art Institute in Los Angeles. It was while she was at school that she met her husband, Lee Blair, the brother of Disney animator Preston Blair. Originally Mary and Lee sought out a career in fine art, but after facing the struggles of that world the two began working for Ub Iwerks, creator of Mickey Mouse, painting animation cels. By 1940 both Mary and Lee were working at the Disney studios doing visual development work for feature films, such as *Dumbo, Lady and the Tramp,* and *Fantasia*. Then, as a part of Franklin D. Roosevelt's Good Neighbor policy, Walt Disney invited a handful of artists on a research tour of South America. Among those artists were Lee and Mary Blair. On that trip Mary became inspired by the color and pattern of the continent. She also quickly became one of Walt's favorite artists in attendance. Upon her return from South America, Mary went on to do visual development for many projects, most notably *Cinderella, Alice in Wonderland*, and *Peter Pan*. Mary then took time off from Disney to raise a family and did advertising work on the side, as well as illustrating many Little Golden Books, including *I Can Fly*. It wasn't until Walt came to Mary with an idea for a ride at his new theme park, Disneyland, in Los Angeles, California, that Mary went back to work for Disney. The ride ultimately became Disney's beloved attraction: It's A Small World, which delights and inspires millions of visitors every year.

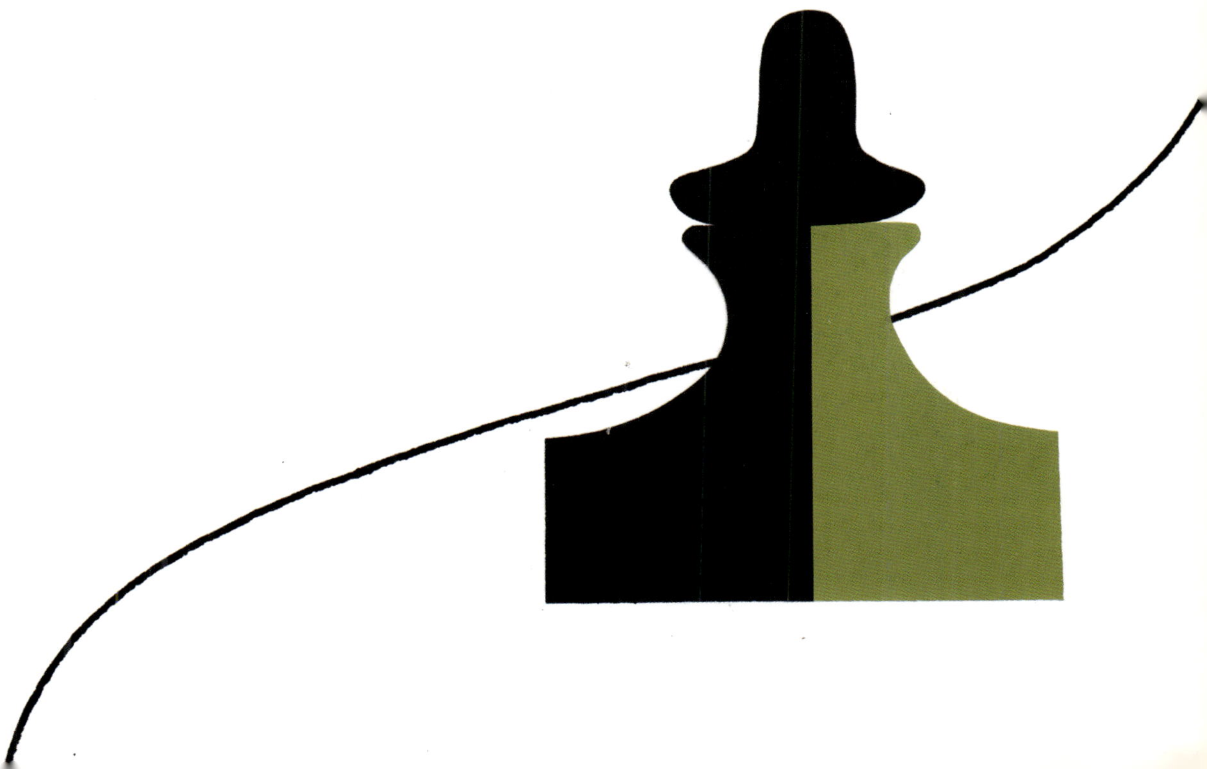

from Ellen Surrey:
for my mother and grandma Jean: two women who always encouraged me to stay true to who I am and pursue my dreams.

from Gloria Fowler:
for my lovely Lola Rae Crist and all her future creative endeavors, and to the memory of her grandmothers Leonor Gaviria Fowler and Donna Lois "Rae" Bentzen Crist.

Illustrated by Ellen Surrey
Edited, written, and art directed by Gloria Fowler

Biographies: Sara DeGonia, Gloria Fowler, Ellen Surrey
Copy Editing: Sara DeGonia
Production: Megan Shoemaker

ISBN: 9781623260828
LOC: 2015943777

Printed in China

For more books and products visit us at:
www.ammobooks.com

AMMO